Mercenary Pilot:
The True Adventures of
"The Doctor"

Table of Contents

That Was Then ...

December 1989:
Woody's Wharf
Newport Beach, California

At the bar in the late afternoon overlooking the Newport Harbor. I was waiting for a real estate friend of mine by the name of Tom to show up with his movie producer friend.

As I drank I noticed a tall, older man at the end of the bar. With his gray hair and goatee, he reminded me of James Colburn in the old movie *Our Man Flint*. He was wearing a powder-blue Armani suit, white shirt, and red tie. Besides making my eyes hurt, I remember thinking the guy looked very out of place, as Woody's was mostly a shorts and T-shirt kind of establishment.

Finally Tom and the producer walked in with a musician friend named Dwight. The four of us sat at the bar discussing my fee for being a ghostwriter and technical adviser on a movie about drug- and gun-running for a to-be-unnamed US government alphabet-soup agency. (The feds never met an acronym or initialism they didn't like. DARPA, ICE, NCIS, DEA, ATF, DOJ, NSA, EIEIO, whatever.)

At one point I got up and was standing by Tom, who was still sitting at the bar. He's looking over my shoulder, and I noticed his eyes getting big. I turned around, and the tall guy was standing right behind me.

Our man Flint said, "Doctor, now is not the time for the book or the movie. You don't want to see your old friends you used to fly for in Central America, now *do you*?

Uh, no, I did not. Thus ended my consulting career before it ever got started.

This Is Now …

2018: Roadhouse Saloon, Palm Springs, CA

I'm sitting at the bar, not a James Colburn doppelganger in sight, thinking about that day in Woody's. Thinking that all my old, lethal friends are either retired, dead, or disappeared. And that movie? Already done and long forgotten.

But also thinking: *Yes, now is finally the perfect time for that book.*

Flashback, 1972

Alongside the Potomac River in Washington, DC, is the sprawling Watergate complex. Opened in 1967 the property houses three apartment buildings, a shopping center, two office buildings, and the luxe Watergate Hotel. Because of its central location, many political organizations rented office space there. The *Melrose Place* of the politico set. In 1972 the Democratic National Committee (DNC)—the primary fund-raising organization for the Democratic Party—also had its headquarters at the Watergate.

On Sunday, May 28, 1972, a team of men working under the cover of darkness broke into the DNC's office. They were not burglars in the normal sense because their intention was not to just steal. Their primary mission was to install wiretaps inside the office of committee chairman Larry O'Brien in order to eavesdrop on his phone calls and office conversations as well as to monitor the activities of the DNC.

Across the street in room 723 of a Howard Johnson's Motor Lodge, the team—later dubbed The Plumbers—spent the next several weeks listening to the wiretaps, hoping to find out who was contributing money to Democrats and any other useful information they could pick up concerning the upcoming presidential election that November. When one of the wiretaps failed, a second mission was ordered.

In the afternoon of June 16, one of the burglars, James McCord, posed as a deliveryman and while in the building taped the locks of stairwell doors up to the sixth floor, where the DNC's offices were located. Mission accomplished, McCord and the others waited for night to fall ...

It had been a typically quiet night when twenty-four-year-old security guard Frank Wills arrived for his midnight shift. Around 1:00 a.m. on June 17, while making his rounds, he noticed someone had taped the lock on one of the stairwell doors, preventing it from automatically locking when shut. When he subsequently found several other doors similarly taped, Wills automatically assumed the cleaning crew was responsible; they often taped the locks or jammed them with paper so they could easily go from floor to floor when cleaning after hours. But the crew was long gone, so Wills removed the tape, made sure the doors were locked, and walked to the Howard Johnson's to grab a cheeseburger ...

When McCord and his four accomplices showed up at the Watergate to replace the malfunctioning bug, they discovered the doors locked. But instead of calling off the mission, he chose to continue. After he had picked the locks and re-taped them, the burglars made their way to the DNC offices …

When Wills returned from his dinner break, he again went on rounds. And again he discovered the stairwell door locks had been jammed. Now he knew for certain this had nothing to do with the cleaning crew. He immediately called his supervisor and the police …

The call came into the Washington, DC, dispatch at 1:52 a.m. A team of three detectives from the tactical squad were immediately dispatched. They followed the trail of taped doors from the basement of the building to the sixth floor where they found the door to the Democratic National Committee had been jimmied. With guns drawn they entered the suite of offices and began to search the rooms one by one. Suddenly, a man jumped up from behind a desk, arms raised over his head, and shouted: "Don't shoot!"

News of the thwarted burglary had Beltway journalists and politicians alike buzzing. Police had apprehended five men, all wearing surgical gloves, carrying $2,300 in $100 bills—their serial numbers in sequence— a bag of sophisticated bugging and burglary equipment, and documents related to strategies for the upcoming national election.

The election committee for then-President Richard Nixon adamantly denied knowledge of wiretapping, and the White House declined comment.

Initially the five burglars gave police false names, but eventually their true identities were established. And that's when the light came on that the Watergate break-in was not merely a random act committed by overzealous Nixon supporters as the White House tried its best to intimate. The men were: Bernard Barker, a former CIA operative now (allegedly) working as a realtor in Miami; Virgilio Gonzales, a Cuban refugee; Eugenio Martinez, who worked for Barker and was also from Cuba; Frank Sturgis, known to have CIA connections; and the group's leader, James McCord, a security advisor for the Republican National Committee and the Committee for the Re-election of the President, amusingly and altogether appropriately known as CREEP. McCord was also a former FBI and CIA agent.

When news of McCord's involvement was released, John Mitchell, the head of CREEP, acknowledged McCord was contracted to provide security services but swore on a non-existent stack of Bibles to the *Washington Post* that the burglars, "were not operating either in our behalf or with our consent. There is no place in our campaign, or in the electoral process, for this type of activity, and we will not permit it nor condone it."

Miraculously, his nose did not grow.

Curiously, neither Mitchell nor anyone else in the RNC admitted to knowing who exactly had hired McCord, when he had been hired, how much he was being paid, or what exactly his responsibilities were. Then there was the matter of their attorneys: high-powered defense lawyers representing "burglars" who apparently had limited means to pay.

What is maybe now the most amazing part of this is that the majority of the public—as well as the press—actually believed the Nixon administration's claims of ignorance and innocence. But back in 1972, most people felt there was no reason *not* to believe the government. As a result, in November 1972 Richard Nixon defeated George McGovern by a landslide. After such a lopsided victory, many in Nixon's White House believed the Watergate incident would eventually blow over.

And it might have, except for those two dogged journalists from the *Washington Post*, Carl Bernstein and Bob Woodward and their covert source Deep Throat. Their reporting on the administration's covert hanky-panky was a shot through the heart of America's political idealism as Bernstein and Woodward exposed one of the greatest presidential scandals in our nation's history.

At least, up till then.

The most important thing about Watergate wasn't that the president was a crook (which he was) or that "former" CIA operatives were conducting nefarious and illegal activities (which they obviously were). The biggest thing is that the American public at large finally got a peek into a lot of shit going on behind the political curtains they hadn't known about. Anyone paying attention would have realized this wasn't an isolated incident; it just happened to be the time these guys got caught.

Nixon resigned in August 1974, just a few years before my friend Ray introduced me into the world of mercenary pilots and the ~~spooks~~ clients they serviced. I would soon learn that 1980s politics, smuggling drugs, gun-running, payoffs, shadow governments, and all those alphabet organizations up to their necks in clandestine missions were the living embodiment of string theory: if you looked deeply enough, you'd see it was all connected. And I'm sure still is.

We might have played a part in the biggest political stories of the 1980s—Iran-Contra, the rise of the Mexican cartels, illegal US involvement in various conflicts—but we weren't part of it. We weren't ideologues. We didn't have a military or political agenda. Nor did we consider ourselves criminals; we were cowboy outlaws, adrenaline junkies seeking adventure and a big payday. I learned early the more cash you have the more you spend, and we religiously spread the wealth at our favorite bars and strip clubs throughout southern Florida and the Caribbean. We were young, we were flush, and we felt immortal—until we weren't.

One last footnote. Remember Frank Wells, the young security guard who nailed the (ahem) burglars? So you'd think he'd parlay his fifteen minutes of fame into at least a better security gig, right?

Nah.

Sure, he got some ink. Newspapers painted him a hero in a modern-day David and Goliath story. An $80 a week African-American security guard alert enough to foil a sophisticated band of suspects. So many reporters wanted to interview Wills that he hired a lawyer/agent and charged a $300 fee for his time, which a few actually paid.

Later the Democratic Party honored him, and he received the Martin Luther King Award from the Southern Christian Leadership Conference. He was even asked to play himself in the movie about Watergate, *All the President's Men,* starring Robert Redford and Dustin Hoffman.

But Frank quickly learned there was a downside to this kind of notoriety. He quit his job with the security firm at the Watergate over a reported dispute about paid vacation days—or more accurately, the lack of any. In 1973 he complained to the *Washington Post* that he was having trouble finding another job with any other security company. Or any company for that matter.

Convinced he was being blackballed by people afraid of and/or in the pocket of those behind the break-in, Frank left DC to live with his ailing mother. Still unemployable, they scraped by on her $450 a month Social Security check. In 1983 he was convicted of shoplifting a pair of tennis shoes and sentenced to a year in jail even though he claimed it had been a misunderstanding. When his mother died, Frank was forced to donate her body to science because he couldn't afford a burial and moved into a shack without electricity or running water.

On the twenty-fifth anniversary of the Watergate break-in, Frank expressed his bitterness in an interview with the *Boston Globe*. "I was doing what I was supposed to do. I was doing my job. And I caught pure hell. I put my life on the line. If it wasn't for me, Woodward and Bernstein would not have known anything about Watergate. This wasn't finding a dollar under a couch somewhere. I never got no kind of commendation.

Nobody invited me to the White House. It will be on my mind until the day I close my eyes."

Which wasn't that long later. Frank died of a brain tumor in 2000. He was just fifty-two years old.

Don't know if there's a moral in this other than messing with the wrong people can be dangerous to your career and your health. This I know from hard-learned experience.

The names of some individuals and government
agencies have been changed ...to protect the guilty.

Chapter One: In the Beginning

I didn't set out to be a pilot growing up. But flying seemed to keep finding me.

In 1974 when I was sixteen years old, all of my buddies were older than me. They were all into cars, so I had a '69 GTO. They were also mostly machinists and mechanics, so that's how I got interested in working on engines and fixing cars.

One of my buddies needed to borrow twenty bucks, so for collateral he gave me a car battery along with a map and an E6B plotter, which is a circular slide-rule pilots use to help navigate. He was taking flying lessons at the time and offered to give me a free lesson. It wasn't as generous as it might seem because the introductory lessons are usually free. They hook you first then charge you.

The plane was a Piper J-3 Cub. It has a simple, lightweight design, so it was easy to handle. It's also one of the most recognizable small propeller planes of all time. My friend never paid me my $20 back, so I just kept taking flying lessons. Of course back then they'd let you fly an airplane by yourself after just eight hours of flight time, which was pretty standard back then. Now it's more like twenty to thirty hours before they let you solo. That also means you started flying bigger planes sooner.

After high school I attended the University of Oregon for a couple of years. I had a friend named Eddy whose father, Rowe, was a flight instructor. One day Rowe said to me, "G, I know you're going to the University of Oregon. I can afford the tuition for Eddy, but I can't afford an apartment. If you let him live with you, then I'll give you flight instruction for free."

So I kept finding myself getting free lessons, and that's how I eventually got all my licenses and commercial ratings. Rowe also had some fun at my expense. Pilot hazing.

One night I show up for training—it was my first night-instrument flight—and he says: "Well, I got a great deal. We got a job hauling a dead body over to Eastern Oregon."

We were transporting it to the mortuary. Back then, it was pretty commonplace, and they still do it today. So Rowe gets in the airplane first then I follow. It's a dark night, and laying in the back of the plane is a body bag complete with dead body. That on its own was creepy enough.

Remember; we're flying in an unpressurized cabin. What I didn't know then as a seventeen-year-old pilot was that as we climbed higher and the pressure became lower, it would have an effect on the gasses in the corpse. I had no idea because this wasn't my usual way to pass a Friday night.

So Rowe is in the right seat, and I'm a brand-new instrument pilot trying to just keep the airplane aloft in the black night sky. We had taken off from Aurora, which is south of Portland, and were gaining altitude when I hear a gurgle and a sound like air coming out of a hose.

Rowe gets this concerned expression. "Oh no. Oh man, we're in big trouble."

I have visions of some catastrophic mechanical problem. "What's wrong? What's happened?"

"I left my gun in the car, the one with the silver bullets in it."

I have no idea what he's talking about. "*What's* the problem?"

He hesitates. "Well, I didn't want to tell you; I didn't want to scare you, but that dead body back there? He died from a werewolf bite."

Right then we hit 12,000 feet, and the body slowly sits up. I mean straight up to almost ninety degrees, and it's gurgling and making all kinds of ungodly sounds. I just about lost my lunch, and I'm man enough to admit I definitely wet my pants. And there's Rowe almost wetting *himself* he's laughing so hard. So that was my initial instrument training experience.

Hardy-fucking-har-har.

Rowe was a memorable guy. We were once in a little Piper Cherokee 140, and he took her into a spin. If you don't know how to get out of a spin, you're not going to survive. I didn't know how and informed him crashing was imminent if he didn't help me out of it.

He says, "Well, you know G, reach up and pull that lightbulb out because it's going to be really dark in that box for a really long time. You don't want to have any regrets."

Not my ideal setting for waxing philosophic. I said, "Yeah, well, I'll ponder that later; now just tell me how to get out of this spin."

He did, and it was forever burned into my memory. But that was his way of training. I don't think they do that too much anymore. There's too much liability; the wings could come off. There's a certain point once the spin tightens where you can't get out. Training is the only time I had to deal with a spin. Truth is, if you get yourself in a spin, you've screwed up by running out of airspeed or something. And you'll almost always pay the ultimate price.

For nonpilots out there, I should explain a bit about certifications. You start out as a student pilot and then after forty hours of flight time— or whatever it is currently—you can apply for your private pilot's license, and there is all kinds of testing for that. The next license is a commercial license then everything else is a rating—the multi-engine rating, the instrument rating—that are added onto your pilot's license. Literally; it's printed right onto the back. The airline transport pilot rating, or ATP certificate, is considered the gold standard.

Now, when you get into bigger jets—anything more than 12,500 pounds—you have to have a *type rating*, so you go to school for a specific airplane, and you get tested specifically on that type of airplane. There are propeller airplanes, there are turboprop planes, and there are jet airplanes. Propeller airplanes are entry level, turboprops and jets are more for corporate and airline use. You need your multi-engine and instrument ratings before you can get into that kind of flying.

As time goes on rules for ratings and certifications are getting stricter. For decades airlines had been able to hire first officers with as little as 250 hours of flight experience and a commercial pilot certificate under their belts. But a new rule put into effect in 2013, requires first officers to have a type rating *and* an ATP with an absolute minimum of 1,500 hours. Fortunately I came up before these new regulations, so I was able to get my ratings when I was pretty young. I got my ATP rating when I was twenty-five, the same year I first flew an Alaska Airlines B-727 jet for my type rating. But that's another story.

I left the University of Oregon after three years and in 1977 enrolled in a community college in Portland to get my aircraft mechanic license, which would take two years. I was living in Salem, about forty-five minutes south of Portland, while going to school. A buddy of mine had a twin-engine airplane and let me fly it as long as I did the maintenance on the plane. I guess I assumed I would make a living working on and maybe flying planes. I just didn't envision exactly how it would shake out.

The Sinner

My cohort in future crime was my friend Ray. We met when we were about seventeen and kind of grew up together flying in Aurora. Rowe, who instructed both of us, one day had said, "I have a guy you gotta meet," and introduced me to Ray.

We were great friends for a lot of years. It was Ray who gave me my name. We all had aliases back then—*nom de vols*, you could say. Ray was the Sinner because he was a really good-looking guy and got all the women; I got all the leftovers.

Ray goes, "So what are we going to call you?"

I just shrugged.

"Well, you'll need a nickname."

I'm not really sure when it happened, but he started calling me the doctor of flight operations, which got shortened to the Doctor.

After the Viet Nam War ended, there were so many former military pilots available, the job market for pilots became tight. As in, there were no jobs to be had here. So Ray went down to Puerto Rico and found work. He was living in a two-bedroom apartment in Isla Verde, a nice suburb of San Juan, and suggested I come down and join him. I could rent out the second bedroom.

I was twenty-two years old and had been flying since 1970. I was a licensed commercial pilot with an instrument and multi-engine rating. I had also gotten my aircraft mechanics licenses (airframe and powerplant). Time to put all that to some use. I decided to move to Puerto Rico and build my flight time for an eventual airline job because pilot jobs were plentiful there, and I had nothing pressing keeping me in Oregon. So I packed my bags and headed for the Caribbean.

The Isle of Enchantment

I flew into San Juan International, and Ray met me at the gate. He drove me to my new digs, and I quickly settled in. It didn't take long to get hired flying a twin-engine, four-passenger Piper Aztec for an air taxi operation based in San Juan. The company transported passengers around Puerto Rico and to the surrounding islands.

Unfortunately, that job was not to last long. A couple of weeks into my employment I was on my final approach to land in St. Thomas and while lowering the landing gear, the nose gear failed to extend. Only the two main wing gears extended. This was obviously a mechanical failure. After exhausting all emergency procedures and checklists to extend the nose gear, it was time to declare an emergency.

One passenger became hysterical when I decided on landing to feather both engines—essentially turning them off so the propellers stop turning—to save the two props and engines from damage. I landed with the nose of the plane sliding to a stop right on the centerline of the runway, saving myself, my passengers, and both engines and props from harm.

My reward from the owner was: "You're fired!"

It was later to be determined that the nose gear's hydraulic actuator had internally failed through no fault of mine. Wouldn't have mattered. It was better optics for the air taxi owner to make it seem like pilot error than plane malfunction.

Job #2

Employment turned out not to be much of a problem. In the weeks to come, I picked up various part-time flying jobs in San Juan.

In the meantime a local Puerto Rican airline hired Ray as a copilot for their fleet of Douglas DC-3s. The company had five, twenty-eight-passenger airliners in service that used a crew of two pilots and one flight attendant. Soon, they were looking for more copilots.

Yippee!

I was hired.

And around that same time the airline promoted Ray to captain, so he and I got to fly together again. It wasn't long before we befriended one of the other copilots I'll call Bob G., who was from a let's-keep-it-unnamed Eastern European country. Bob was an excellent pilot and highly respected within the airline. He was the only copilot given a left-seat authorization, meaning he could fly from the captain's seat—which is located on the left—when he operated the aircraft. But Bob could not legally check out as captain because he was too young. You had to be twenty-one or older to get an ATP certificate.

My Introduction to Mercenary Flying

The airline didn't fly at night, so that's when all crew training was done. At the time there were no DC-3 simulators to train on.

Crew training usually consisted of multiple hours with multiple crew members night flying to the various islands. Making it more fun was that there was zero air traffic control back then except for San Juan International, and we were out of their control range. Meaning, we couldn't talk to them. The San Juan Int. airport control tower and various airport agencies became used to this over the years, and most government agencies were off duty at night.

One night I was home at the apartment watching TV around 2:00 a.m. Ray seemed to be missing in action, so I assumed he must be doing some unscheduled flight training since the airline had recently promoted him to chief pilot. I was soon to find out *unscheduled* didn't quite cover it.

I was still awake when Ray showed up around 3:00 a.m. He walked into the kitchen/dining room dressed in his full captain's uniform, carrying a rather large gym bag. He tossed it on the table and unzipped it.

Like a scene out of a movie, it was full of cash.

As Capt. Ray told it, his first official act as chief pilot was to cancel all training that night. He then, uhm, ~~appropriated~~ ~~borrowed~~ ~~temporarily~~ ~~stole~~ liberated one of the company's aircraft. He had left in the afternoon on a training flight plan then Capt. Ray proceeded to Colombia by himself.

Upon arrival in South America's drug cartel capital of the world, the plane's cabin was loaded with product. Conveniently, the backs of the passenger seats would fold forward and flat. Capt. Ray didn't say where he stopped to unload before returning to San Juan Int. Nor did he say how he got hooked up although I assumed it was through some of the shadier characters working at the airline.

What he did say was, "That was one long-ass flight, and I could sure use a co-pilot next time."

And that's how the adventures began.

Soon after that, the nonsked airline came to its expected conclusion.

It went bankrupt.

Aviation History 101

Nonsked, or non-scheduled, airlines began after World War II when the military started selling its surplus planes to private buyers. The planes were generally sold cheap, and aviation entrepreneurs created small, independent airlines for cargo and passenger transport. Many of the buyers were former fighter pilots who wanted to continue flying but couldn't—or didn't want to—make it as passenger airline pilots for whatever reason (disliked corporate environments, thought the uniforms itched, couldn't pass the drug test, wanted to pick their own work hours, made more money flying contraband—take your pick.) So instead they flew cargo or started independent passenger flights.

The Civil Aeronautics Authority—the predecessor to the FAA—dictated that these independents couldn't have any regularly scheduled routes, so they improvised. They competed against the five or six major airlines that existed at the time by offering lower prices and the willingness to fly whatever, wherever.

That lack of scheduling was why these small airlines were dubbed nonsked. In the United States, after about fifteen years of operation, the CAA essentially regulated many of these small airlines out of business.

Somebody had to fill the void. (Mercenary pilots, at your service...)

Capt. Ray and the Doctor's First Adventure

During the airline smuggling operation, Ray and I had made some fast friends at and around the airport. Definitely not the kind of guys you'd want your daughter or sister to go out with. Some were pilots and some were not. But they all had ongoing operations on the dark side of the airport ramp in San Juan.

We'd finish one operation, and it wouldn't be long before Ray and I were back at the controls for another. We were now extremely well-versed in borrowing aircraft—usually large aircraft of the DC-3 and Convair CV-440 variety.

True fact: Convair later expanded into rockets and spacecraft, manufacturing the first Atlas rockets, including those used for the manned-flights of Project Mercury. Super cool.

We'd also borrow an occasional Buffalo aircraft, DC-4 or DC-6, for fun and profit.

After all, we were mercenaries, the new Pirates of the Caribbean! We were young and invincible! Remember how bulletproof you felt at that age? (These days I seem to have misplaced my bulletproof underwear. But I digress.) We were making wads of cash and spending just as much. It was fun and exciting and life was good.

What could possibly go wrong?

Ray and me in Puerto Rico

Flashback, 1980

In the United States the new decade ushered out the flamboyance of the '70s and Jimmy Carter's liberal idealism and ushered in the Moral Majority that helped sweep Ronald Reagan into office. The new president's belief that communism anywhere threatened democracy everywhere would lead to an environment rife with ideologues where illegal black ops to further unsanctioned military and political objectives thrived.

In the Middle East Saddam Hussein ordered his forces to invade Western Iran. That war would last most of the decade, causing more than one million military and civilian casualties. The US government's support of Iran, the lesser of two political evils, later played a critical role in some notorious alphabet agency covert activity in Central America designed to aid the Contra rebels' efforts to overthrow Nicaragua's communist Sandinista government, a conflict that would keep many mercenary pilots busy and rolling in the green for years.

Against that under-the-radar political intrigue, 1980 was also a year of cultural and social milestones. John Lennon is shot and killed in New York by a killer obsessed with Jodie Foster. Post-It Notes arrived. Racial tensions run high in Miami rioting. The MGM Grand Hotel in Las Vegas catches on fire, killing eighty-five people. Camcorders and fax machines are introduced in Japan. Pac-Man is released. Six months after the Miracle on Ice at the Winter Olympics, the United States boycotts the Summer Games in Moscow. The world tunes in to find out who shot JR on *Dallas*. Mount St. Helens erupts. CNN debuts as the world's first twenty-four-hour news channel.

The stock market reached 963, the average cost of new house was $68,700, and an American's average income was $19,500.

I guarantee you, mercenary pilots earned much, much more.

Chapter Two: Flying for Pepe

Ray and I started flying for a major provider of Colombian product in Puerto Rico. We called him Pepe. He was overall a great guy. Although he was the size of Jabba the Hutt, Pepe was all about having fun and revelled in throwing extravagant parties.

Ray and I flew several errands for Pepe. After one such trip Pepe owed us a rather large sum of *dinero*. So one day we got a phone call at our base of operation, otherwise known as poolside at the El San Juan Hotel and Casino in Isla Verdi.

We were instructed to meet Pepe's lieutenants out on a rarely-used dirt road in the middle of nowhere. It was infamous for being a body dump site. And yes, this gave us pause.

So I put both of my fully automatic Mac 11 .45 calibers with Sonic silencers attached and twenty thirty-round clips in the back seat of our rental car. In the trunk were one thousand rounds still in the cardboard box they came in. Suitably armed, Ray and I drove down Baity Realty Road a couple of miles then came to a stop, surrounded by empty fields. It wasn't long before a white, four-door Chevy Impala, about a 1966 vintage, pulled up behind us.

Ray was driving, so I said, "If they get out, we'll take off."

Well, four young Puerto Ricans got out, and Ray floored it. We got about one hundred yards ahead of them before they jumped back into their car and started chasing us. I told Ray to pull over and stop. He did.

I pulled both Mac 11s from the back seat then locked and loaded them. I was standing behind our rental car as the Impala pulled up. The four young lieutenants got out and cleared the car. I let go with both Macs straight up the front of their hood and windshield. It looked like a couple of perforated racing stripes.

Needless to say, they took off on a dead run down the dirt road.

Ray and I got the rounds out of the trunk and proceeded to put a .45 bullet hole in every inch of the car, using up the entire box. When we finished, there was a solid ring of brass all the way around the car.

We returned to our hotel to find the red light blinking on our phone. Pepe had left us a message: *Your money is in the hotel safe. Come to my house tonight. I'm having a party in your honor.*

Not being fearless, I tucked my Smith and Wesson .357 mag into my right Tony Lama cowboy boot then set off with Ray. When we got to his house, Pepe opened the front door himself. Inside a full-blown party was in progress complete with DJ. On a scale of one to bacchanalia, it was at least a nine.

As we walked through the front door, Pepe pointed to three young Puerto Rican guys hanging from a ceiling beam in the living room, strung up by chains. Mouths and ankles duct-taped, they were clothed only in their underwear. All over the house people were dancing and parting, oblivious and/or unconcerned about this spectacle in their midst.

Pepe handed Ray and I each an aluminum baseball bat. "They are your piñatas."

I asked Pepe what was going on.

"They were going to kill you guys to save me money by not having to pay you!"

These were obviously not the four sharpest knives in the butcher block. "Did you tell them you made one hundred times what you paid us?" I asked.

"Oh, no. I couldn't tell them that," he laughed. "Then they would want a pay raise."

I tried handing him back the bat. "Well, cut them down and release them."

He raised his hands and shook his head. "I can't do that; I'll lose face!"

I held out the bat again. "If you don't, I'm done flying for you."

With a pouty sigh Pepe told one of his lieutenants. "Okay, cut them down and let them go."

I've never seen three guys in their underwear run that fast down out the door and down the road. Then it occurred to me what was wrong with that picture.

"Hey, Pepe; where's the fourth guy?"

He pooched out his lips and pointed them toward the pool outside. (Pointing with one's lips is a ubiquitous Puerto Rican gesture.)

I followed his glance and saw the fourth guy in the pool also wearing just underwear. He was also sporting fresh bullet holes, floating face down, with party-goers walking by nonchalantly.

I stared at Pepe. He shrugged. "I had to save face, you know?"

We didn't stay long.

One Month Later

Despite the party from hell, we were still flying for Pepe. I was on an operation in Costa Rica where I had broken one of my rules: never take friends on missions. But I had a roommate that was between jobs who really needed the money. We called him Ski Bob because he was an ex-ski instructor. In San Juan, Puerto Rico. Obviously, not much call for ski instructors on the island. Ski Bob was also an ex-door gunner and crew chief in Vietnam and very capable.

Our team was operating out of San Jose, Costa Rica. After a few days in the country, Ski Bob and I went downtown for a cocktail; as usual, we were mighty thirsty. We were also unarmed.

Stupid.

We partied hard at a place called Leonardo's Disco Club. It's still there. After leaving, Ski Bob and I noticed we'd overserved ourselves. By a lot. We were standing in the street in front of the club when we were confronted by three, armed Costa Ricans.

In the best of situations, this is not ideal. But before we could process our lack of options, the bandits abruptly dropped their weapons, turned, and ran away.

I turned to Ski Bob. "Well, one of us must have scared them. And I know it wasn't me."

We looked behind us to see three young Puerto Ricans standing behind us, heavily-armed with AK-47s. Through my alcohol haze I recognized them. They were the lieutenants I had Pepe cut down and release at his house. Without a word they stepped back into the darkness, never to be seen again while we were in Costa Rica.

When later querying Pepe about this, he laughed. "They have been following you ever since their release to make sure you're safe because they owe you their lives."

I had never noticed them. It was both comforting and not.

The Failed Trip to Colombia

Getting back to work in Costa Rica, Ski Bob and I were prepping for our upcoming mission, and I was supervising some aircraft maintenance being done by Copa SA aviation there. I had experience working on the Convair 440s Pratt & Whitney R-2800-CB 16 engines, which were the same engines as on the DC-6.

The rest of our crew had just arrived in San Jose. The first officer was a Puerto Rican national named Al, a good friend we called the Super Ratón, which some translated as *Big Rat,* but it really means *Mighty Mouse.* We had flown together a lot over the past few years. The Convair's real mechanic, Moisase, also Puerto Rican, had arrived with our Cuban radio operator who was in charge of the communications center in the aircraft, which included a high frequency radio and three ham radios: a 40 meter (7-MHz band), allocated to radio amateurs worldwide; a 20 meter (14-MHz band), considered among the best for long-distance communication; and a 2 meter, reserved exclusively for those licensed by the FCC as amateur radio operators. Ski Bob was our acting crew chief and co-kicker along with Moisase.

And what, you may wonder, is a kicker? They toss the product out of the plane to the waiting boats in the ocean below. Always at night.

Taking Off

It was time to start the op, and all seemed in order. When flight planning these excursions, I like to start with at least an 80 percent chance of success because I've learned over the years that as soon as you take off and get wheels up, your success rate drops to half. Then it usually goes downhill from there. That's just the nature of the beast.

On takeoff from San Jose, the weather was bad, requiring instrument flight rules. This was before GPS was standard equipment, so with some high terrain in the area and poor navigational aids, we were not planning to return to San Jose.

The weather down south was forecast to be good. I had filed a phony flight plan from Costa Rica to St. Martin. I purposely underestimated the aircraft speed, endurance (fuel burn), and fuel on board, meaning we could fly faster and further in reality than what I'd indicated. The plan was to fly from Costa Rica to a covert dirt airstrip in Colombia where we would refuel and load product. Then we'd fly to the drop zone, make the airdrop, then land in St. Martin. Piece of cake, you say? Ha!

Murphy's Law: Anything that can go wrong, will go wrong.

Words to live by when you're a mercenary.

Well, we made it to Colombia, even found the strip without radio contact. But nobody was there, and it was too dangerous to land without talking to someone on the ground by radio because the military would routinely string large steel cables across the runway. So Houston, we had a problem and a huge decision to make. We didn't have enough fuel to make it to St. Martin, and the weather in Costa Rica was too treacherous to return. Landing at the nearest island, Aruba, meant six weeks in jail before you even saw an attorney. That was definitely not an option!

So we decided to head to Panama.

We radioed Cinimer—Central America air traffic control—and relayed that we had been en route from Costa Rica to St. Martin when we suffered an engine failure but couldn't return to Costa Rica due to weather. We received clearance to land at Panama city's main airport.

On short approach to the runway, I feathered the right engine to appear it had failed. After landing we were instructed to taxi to the military ramp and park

Hmm, I thought. *This is not the usual protocol.*

After parking and shutting down, the plane was surrounded by three military armored personnel carriers (APC).

Oh, yes. The party was definitely over.

When we deplaned, we were informed by the military that our Convair 440 had been involved in several "*Midnight Express* trips," and we were immediately arrested. So for the next three days and nights, we were the guests of the Panamanian government.

The first day started with our interrogation by none other than Col. Manuel Noriega, the notorious strongman. Before installing himself as dictator—the previous leader had died in a suspicious 1981 plane crash—Noriega had run military intelligence. But he couldn't speak a lick of English. So he brought the airport tower operator, who spoke very good English and was also a private pilot, into the interrogation to act as an interpreter.

When the tower operator walked past me, I slipped a $100 bill into his pocket. He didn't look to see the denomination, so maybe it was just the thought that counted. He studied our flight plan then did all the calculations based on that and the (falsified) performance info I gave him.

The tower operator then told Noriega, "They couldn't have been anywhere else than where they said they were."

The colonel was pissed, jumping up and down, smacking his riding crop on the table, screaming, *"Están mintiendo!"* (They're lying!)

Mind you, Manuel was about my height (translation: short), so he looked like a (psychotic) toddler having a tantrum. I kept that observation to myself.

After day three even the colonel had no reason to hold us, so we were released. We did not pass go or collect $200. We went straight to the aircraft, and as the crew and I were preparing to go, I noticed Col. Noriega's jeep on the right side of the Convair just off the taxiway.

I said to Super Ratón, "You make the takeoff from the left seat; I'll be in the right seat. I have something to do."

As we rolled down the runway past the Jeep, I opened the right copilot window, pulled my pants down, and stuck my bare ass out the window in front of Noriega.

It didn't go unnoticed.

On the climb out from Panama, we all had a great laugh about that. But our levity was short-lived; we soon realized we had left Panama too early at 10:00 a.m. The runway at San Jose International was closed until noon because of runway maintenance. We only had an hour's worth of fuel, just enough to fly to Costa Rica. No way we could circle the airport and wait for it to reopen. We had to turn around and go back to Panama.

Mierda.

Upon our return and landing, we were once again instructed to park on the now familiar military ramp. Then comes Noriega's staff car with the little flags attached to the front fenders.

I'm thinking: *We are definitely going to get shot.*

The car pulls up and the door opens. It's the tower guy. And he's laughing.

"Nice show. It's your lucky day. The colonel's daughter has a horse-riding show that he had to attend, but he will be back soon. And this time he *will* shoot you. I have a guard at the front gate that will call when the colonel returns. Then you have to go."

When he got the call, we left.

The Midget

It was a short, uneventful trip to San Jose. Until we arrived.

While taxiing we noticed about ten people lined up along the side of the runway. After we parked a midget—not a nickname, the actual condition—and a behemoth Costa Rican boarded the aircraft. The midget explained they were all from the Costa Rican narcotics division and he—the midget—was in charge.

The midget instructed us to taxi to a remote ramp at the airport where they, the narcotics division, would search the aircraft. The midget deplaned, leaving the Costa Rican Paul Bunyan to keep an eye on us.

We fired up the bird and started to taxi, with the not-so-jolly giant standing behind my seat. To get to the remote ramp, we had to taxi onto the runway.

(Aha, you say.)

As we turned onto the runway, in true Puerto Rican style, I pointed to the water injection switch with my lips. Super Ratón, sitting in the right seat, turned the switch on. When the blue armed light came on, I pushed the throttles up to takeoff power. That's when super-sized standing behind me pulled out a .45 automatic and put the gun to the right side of my head.

So much for that plan.

I immediately pulled the power and water injection off then parked the Convair 440 on the ramp. Now the fun was about to start. The midget arrived with the rest of his crew and instructed them to tear into everything inside and out. And tear into it they did. The aircraft was in a freighter/cargo configuration, meaning there were no seats in the cabin. Also, the restroom and toilet holding tank had been removed along with the clean-out valve next to the outside toilet dump receptacle.

As the midget's crew ripped the aircraft apart in search of narcotics, I noticed the midget was watching me. Whenever I looked at a section of the aircraft, he would have his minions tear into that section. Testing my theory, I looked at the tires, thinking that would be the only place they wouldn't look. Nope. The midget yelled at his crew to jack up the plane and pull off the tires. But they didn't have big enough jacks. Ha!

So seeing that, the Super Ratón and I ganged up on the midget. We both stood by the rear right side of the Convair 440 and stared at the toilet clean-out receptacle. The midget took the bait. He walked over and grabbed the clean-out cap and started turning it to open, all the time looking back at me.

I told him in Spanish, *"Te van a cubrir de mierde,"* (You're going to get covered in shit) as I—and his entire team—moved back.

The midget chickened out and didn't open it.

He was pissed, but we were released shortly after that. I told the midget we were going to be partying at my favorite club that night, Leonardo's, in downtown San Jose.

"Come on down."

Later, at Leonardo's …

My crew and I were partying hard when the midget and four of his henchmen showed up at the club. I invited them to join the crew. We were drinking Cristal champagne, smoking Cuban cigars, and quaffing hot Costa Rican ladies.

The midget says, "You know I was only doing my job. I had to make it look good for the locals. But we're partners."

I nodded. "Cool."

"If you tell me where you hide the stuff on the aircraft, I won't look there next time."

I thought, *ha.* I said, "Okay, but since I don't know you or trust you yet, you pick up the entire bar bill tonight for all of us. Deal?"

He paid the entire $2,500 bar bill.

Sucker.

I said, "Well, when I get home I'll send you a postcard saying where we keep the stuff."

He eagerly said okay.

True to my word I sent him a lovely postcard of a sunset with the message: *Yes, the plane was loaded, and you missed it. It was in the shitter tank, and if you had opened the dump cap, you would have found it.*

In truth there had been nothing on the plane because we'd never been able to land in Columbia. I just wanted to get his goat. And I knew that the next time a Convair 440 came through San Jose, the midget may or may not open that dump cap and get shit all over him.

And no, I haven't been back to Costa Rica since.

The Aero Commander Affair

As Ray and I expanded our operation, we took on a new client by the name of Chino. He was a native Puerto Rican but got his nickname because he looked Chinese. He was a great guy full of energy. Chino lived modestly in a poor community on the outskirts of San Juan and just wanted to use his ill-gotten gains to help his friends, family, and the surrounding community. He imported Colombian product and like Pepe wanted a better life for himself and his countrymen.

Ray and I were doing *very* well by this time and had just acquired a turboprop Aero Commander 680V. An old aircraft by modern standards but right up our alley: it was expendable and cheap.

This adventure started at Burbank airport in Southern California. Ray and I brought along a good friend of ours who I'll call Triple X, a surfer who liked big waves. We departed from Burbank en route to Puerto Rico, with a scheduled fuel stop along the way, then an overnight in Miami. But when we reached Florida, the aircraft suffered an engine instrument failure. So we put the 680V in maintenance at an Aero Commander service center—a fixed base operation, which means it's allowed to operate at the airport to provide aeronautical services—then called it a night.

The next day we got a ridiculous $13,000 bill for an engine gauge and labor, which probably worked out to $3750 an hour.

Talk about mercenary ...

So we came up with a plan to steal our own aircraft, which was locked up at the hangar. Aviation dine-and-dash!

At the service center Ray approached a technician—a nice elderly gentleman—and explained that he had accidentally left his medication onboard. He asked if he could unlock the aircraft to get it.

The technician gave Ray a key made from an old Ford blank. "I used to work at the Aero Commander factory, and that's a master key that will open all Aero Commanders, so please bring it right back."

Well, Ray brought it right back—after making ten copies—and we successfully liberated the Aero Commander without paying for the overpriced repair.

Free is good.

We flew from Miami International to San Juan, Puerto Rico. But after a hard night partying in Miami, we had neglected to get any maps, and returning certainly wasn't an option. We managed to find a *National Geographic* magazine with a map of the Caribbean. Good enough.

After landing in Puerto Rico, we checked back into our base of operations: the El San Juan Hotel and Casino in Isla Verde. It wasn't long before Chino had a mission for us, and we were invited to his small ranch-style house out in the mountainous countryside for lunch and flight planning. He lived with his wife and a young Doberman named Little Ricky.

We were partying hard at Chino's house, as you do. Walking through the kitchen on the way to the bathroom, I noticed smoke coming from the cabinet below the kitchen sink. Thinking there was a fire, I opened the cabinet doors and instead found an array of lit candles illuminating several voodoo dolls with pins stuck all over them.

I casually queried Chino about this. "You are aware there are candles and voodoo dolls stashed under the kitchen sink, yes?"

"Ah, yes. My wife is a voodoo high priestess. She is working on eliminating the competition."

I wondered if it would work on pilots.

Anyway, the deal was sealed. But Ray and I decided to take a break and let Triple X take the trip.

In the meantime two old pilot friends—mine and Ray's old flight instructor Rowe and one of his training students, Danny—showed up in San Juan looking for some adventure and profit. Rowe had met Danny while flight instructing in the Midwest. Danny had a private pilot's license but no instrument or multi-engine ratings yet.

The trip from San Juan to Colombia and back was scheduled and flight-planned. Triple X would be the captain and Danny would be the copilot. On go-day we loaded 150 gallons of jet fuel in ten-gallon military cans into the aircraft cabin for the return trip to San Juan—I love the smell of jet fuel in the morning—then said good-bye, and they left.

Upon arrival on the Guajira peninsula in northeast Colombia at night and unknown to Capt. Triple X, the local Wayuu Indians had dug a trench across the runway about a third of the way down.

Bummer.

Apparently the Wayuu had not been compensated for the use of their airstrip by the time Triple X and Danny got there, which resulted in the separation of the left main gear from the aircraft upon hitting the trench when landing. Without the left main gear to support the aircraft, the left engine hit the ground and caught fire. The right engine fuel controller was damaged on impact and went to max power, causing the aircraft to veer off the runway and impact the jungle.

Double bummer.

With the Aero Commander now on fire and burning in the Columbian jungle, Triple X and Danny somehow managed to rescue all 150 gallons of jet fuel before it became a marshmallow roast.

Ray and I got the call around 2:00 a.m. on the 40-meter ham radio set up in our hotel room.

I asked Triple X, "What do I need to bring down to fix the plane?"

"I had to use the Bic lighter on it."

The protocol in Colombia is if the aircraft is disabled and can't leave before your time slot runs out---usually four hours—you burn it then bury it.

Bye-bye Aero Commander; we hardly knew ya.

The next day the military found the smoking wreckage at the remote strip with no pilot bodies. The search for them was on. Triple X and Danny spent the next couple of days hiding out in the closest city, Riohacha, but their time would be running out. So a rescue mission was mounted with Ray, me, and a new arrival and associate, Mr. K, because Rowe had chickened out.

The Plan

There was a brand-new turboprop Aero Commander 1000 on the ramp in San Juan International. Since we had a master key, courtesy of the trusting gent in Miami, we were going to borrow it. But neither Ray nor I knew how to fly this new generation of Turboprop, so we broke into the aircraft at night and ~~stole~~ borrowed the flight manual. We also checked the fuel quantity to be sure we could to make it to Colombia, and we could. And we had the 150 gallons of jet fuel in Colombia for our return, so we were looking good.

We studied the flight manual through the night and all the next day. The plan was to grab the bird that night. We had a momentary scare later when we checked on the plane, and it was gone. Luckily it returned the same day; we assumed the owner had flown to St. Thomas to stock up on booze.

So the mission was on. We radioed Triple X we were coming that night so they could plan the six-hour drive—mostly on trails requiring four-wheel drive—from Riohacha back to the landing strip.

Ray, Mr. K, and I unlocked the Aero Commander 1000. To our dismay the owner had not refueled the aircraft after returning from wherever, and now we didn't have enough fuel to make it to Colombia.

Bummer squared.

We had no option but to taxi the bird to the refueling pits and called for fuel. Ray and I were far too well-known at the airport, so we dressed up Mr. K in Ray's pilot uniform, which was at least one size too small. Although Mr. K was not a pilot, he pulled it off no problem. The fuel bill was around $1,500. Mr. K gave them $2,000 cash and said have a nice day.

With all of us wearing surgical gloves to avoid leaving tell-tale fingerprints, we flew to Colombia that night, made radio contact with Triple X, and the Colombian crew lit up the dirt strip with low-light smudge pots.

Triple X radioed, "You might want to land a little long and miss that trench across the runway."

Ya think?

Everyone was busy. The Colombians were loading product—we still had to bring home the bacon even on a rescue mission—and our crew was loading jet fuel. All was going well until the gasoline-powered car fuel pump we were using to pump the jet fuel ran out of gas. Before we could address this conundrum, one of the Colombian crew filled the automobile gas pump with jet fuel. That was the end of the pump.

So now our crew was fueling by hand, pouring jet fuel in the over-wing fuel ports. This was very time consuming, and we were running out of our allotted time slot. The protocol there is that the Colombian Air Force colonel gets paid $40,000, and you get a four-hour time slot. If you exceed that, you're fair game. Well, we exceeded that, and it was game on as we could see the distant lights of military helicopters approaching.

On climb out we could see machine gun tracer rounds in the night sky flashing past the aircraft's windows, but we quickly out-climbed them. The 1000 Aero Commander saved us.

But there went one of my nine lives.

All five of us and a large quantity of product had made it onboard. We don't drink and fly, but I found a jar of shelled sunflower seeds and passed it around. We did spill a fair share of them on the floor.

We landed on a short remote strip about one mile from San Juan International, where we unloaded product and crew, with the exception of Triple X and Danny. They were to fly the Aero Commander to another remote runway on the other side of the island and abandon it, which they did.

Unfortunately for the Aero Commander 1000 owner, the local Drug Enforcement Agency office discovered the aircraft before the owner knew it was missing and could report it stolen. The police and DEA agents surrounded his house and arrested him, announcing in their exuberance that they had found "marijuana seeds" all over the floor.

Once someone bothered to look more closely at their evidence, he was released and not charged.

To the Aero Commander 1000 owner:

Please take solace knowing your aircraft helped save the lives

of two people, and we are eternally grateful. Thank you, -

The Doctor

Ray and Danny, RIP

That same year we lost both Ray and Danny.

Danny wasn't the sharpest tool in the box. A serious weightlifter, he looked like the Incredible Hulk. That being said, Danny was a great guy and well-liked by everyone he met, and he did stand out in a crowd.

One time Ray and I saw Danny getting into a straight-tail twin Bonanza. But we knew he was not rated for multi-engine piloting, so we got him out of the plane. It turned out Danny had falsified his FAA license by typing the multi-engine and instrument ratings on the front of it himself—the licenses were made of paper back them—and had persuaded Chino to let him fly a solo trip.

Stupid, stupid, stupid.

Ray and I later warned Chino not to let Danny fly solo as he was in no way qualified for our type of flying.

Well, as they say, stupid is as stupid does.

When Ray and I were on a mission in a land far, far away, Danny liberated a corporate aircraft belonging to a major local Puerto Rican drug manufacturer, a twin-engine Beechcraft Barron. We can only guess at what might have happened. The most likely scenario was that Danny made it to Colombia during daylight hours then tried to return at night. But the Barron, now loaded with product, would be much heavier, so it would burn a lot more fuel on the return trip. Also he would be returning at night and regardless of what was typed on his license, he was not instrument rated. So did he run out of fuel, lose control of the aircraft at night, suffer engine failure, or simply get lost until he ran out of fuel and sank into the deep blue sea?

While the Coast Guard did find some of the wreckage floating in the ocean, Danny's body was never recovered.

So stupid.

Ray was a different story.

He and I had begun taking turns flying smaller, twin-engine aircraft on the more dangerous missions. It was my turn to fly, and it was going to be an extremely hazardous trip.

Then on the day of the go-night, Ray approached me and announced, "Doctor, I'm flying this trip."

Although I did register my complaint, it was futile. There was a pecking order and with Ray the senior pilot, I had no choice but to accept his directive.

Ray took off from San Juan International for Colombia then was to return and land on a dirt road in the middle of a sugarcane field on the other side of the island. Again, all at night. I would be waiting for his return with a remote radio, ready to light up the dirt road with smudge pots and the rental car's headlights. I waited a long time.

Ray never returned.

I learned that Ray had made it to Colombia during daylight hours and apparently had a flight instrument failure on the way. There was a Colombian aircraft mechanic on the strip, but as the story goes Ray didn't trust him. But Ray was not an aircraft mechanic, and he was returning to Puerto Rico at night and would need those flight instruments to get back.

The last thing he said to the boss in charge of the covert strip before his departure was, "I got this one."

Along with Super Ratón, I flew the Convair 440 on search trips but to no avail. Ray was never seen or heard from again, and this time no wreckage was ever found. Personally, I like to think he was abducted by aliens and is showing the ETs how to *party*!

But in the void he left behind, it was hard not to have some *it could have been me* thoughts, since it was supposed to be my flight. So with Ray's demise, I felt another one of my lives had gone with him.

Flashback, 1982

Play a word association game with your average John Q public (wo)man on the street by saying *Colombia, South America*, and odds are their immediate response will either be cocaine, cartel, or Pablo Escobar. Since the later 1970s Colombia has achieved international notoriety as a major narcotics trafficking center. But the country's involvement with drugs had been a national pastime long before Americans took notice. Consider that Colombia's indigenous populations have grown and chewed coca plants for thousands of years. It just took a while for the rest of the world to catch on.

Marijuana cultivation, in contrast, has been a much more recent phenomenon and flew more under the radar than its splashier, look-at-me powdered cousin. The cannabis market arrived in Colombia along the Caribbean coast via Panama during the very early 1900s. By the 1930s, limited cultivation had begun among the Costeño population in Barranquilla, located in Northern Colombia, where urban *traquetos* (mid-level drug dealers) routinely smoked the local cannabis.

During World War II, experiments with hemp cultivation designed to increase fiber production for the war effort, substantially expanded its cultivation. (Thanks, Uncle Sam!) But the real takeoff of Colombian marijuana production began in the mid- to late-1960s, driven by the growing demand of American users. Blame the tuning in, turning on, dropping out Hippies.

By the early 1970s, Colombia had emerged as a major United States weed supplier, although most of the market remained in the hands of Mexican middlemen traffickers. When the DEA tightened up drug enforcement along the United States-Mexican border in the early 1970s, the Mexican state launched a major pogrom against its domestic producers, and the epicenter of marijuana production in the Northern Hemisphere rapidly shifted to Colombia, specifically to the Guajira Peninsula (RIP Aero Commander) and the slopes of the Sierra Nevada de Santa Marta.

By the end of the decade, Colombia accounted for about 70 percent of all marijuana coming into the United States from abroad. It might have been entertainment and snack-food munchies heaven for American pot heads, but for between thirty- to fifty-thousand small farmers along Colombia's Caribbean coast, it was their cash crop, while at least another fifty-thousand Colombians—seasonal pickers, transporters, guards, and bankers—made a living from it.

The trade proved to be an important source of new wealth for the Caribbean coast, providing the population with income, comforts, and a degree of economic stability that they had never enjoyed before. The Caribbean port cities of Barranquilla, Santa Marta, and Riohacha in particular, experienced unprecedented prosperity. That was the good news.

The bad news was that the Guajira Peninsula experienced a dramatic upsurge in drug-related violence along with municipal police and judicial corruption. Local food production declined as tens of thousands of acres of agricultural land were converted to marijuana cultivation. Farmers engaged in growing traditional crops such as bananas found labor more expensive and in short supply. Inflation soared as drug barons bid up prices. Many legitimate businesses, including banks, hotels, airlines, restaurants, and casinos, were bought up by the syndicates and used for laundering illicit profits.

Pick your poison.

As cocaine use in the United States exploded in the 1970s, it became DEA public enemy number one. The ruthless and vicious Medellín and Cali drug cartels made the old New York Mafia's exploits look quaint by comparison. Their leaders, including Pablo Escobar, believed themselves to be untouchable by the law. And they were pretty much right for a long time, thanks to paying millions in bribes to law enforcement officials in Colombia, the United States, and elsewhere for protection.

By the early 1980s the marijuana pipeline flow was quickly being eclipsed by the cocaine trade in terms of the wealth and power associated with it. But it's all relative; one mercenary's pocket change is another's pot of gold. Cannabis was a steady, sought-after, relatively lower-risk commodity. And people who smoke weed are generally less amped and testy than those who fuel themselves on powder, so you were marginally less likely to encounter someone who'd been up for days wanting to introduce you to their little friend.

We've all seen *Scarface*.

But the ongoing marijuana trade plus the cocaine activity caught the attention not only of the DEA but of other alphabet-soup agencies who were/are always on the lookout for opportunities to further their own agendas. That meant life was getting decidedly more complicated and certainly riskier for your everyday working stiff mercenary pilots.

If you weren't careful, you could go through your nine lives awfully quickly

Chapter Three: Mr. T and the Super Ratón

Enter Mr. T. In reality I had known Mr. T for as long as I had known Al, the Super Ratón. Mr. T and Al were partners in a legitimate cargo airline operating a Convair 440 aircraft out of San Juan International Airport. While I was still flying for the now-defunct DC-3 airline, I flew occasional trips as a copilot for Mr. T when Al couldn't make it.

Mr. T became one of my best friends and golfing partners. We both joined the beautiful Rio Mar Country Club located in Rio Grande an hour from San Juan. We played beer golf; that's when you suck at golf—which we did—so you drink beer while playing and don't keep score. We had a great time, and the only danger at the club was getting a sunburn.

Mr. T was an excellent pilot; one of the best I've seen. He tried to stay on the up-and-up, flying only legal cargo runs. But between over-competition and Eastern Airlines hauling more belly freight to the outer islands, the independent cargo market share all but dried up. By then I was flying for some major players in Medellín, Colombia, and had earned the reputation of getting the job done.

So in stepped the Doctor with a proposition he couldn't refuse.

Mr. T joined the crew as the new *el capitán*. On flights he joined either Super Ratón or me or both of us along with Moisase the mechanic plus a radio operator, crew chief, and kicker as needed.

As usual, it wasn't long before our services were needed. And it happened to be a trip for my old friend Pepe.

The Plan

Pepe set it up so that Mr. T and I would arrive via a proper airline in Barranquilla, Colombia, posing as boxing promoters looking to arrange a bout between a well-known Puerto Rican boxer and a well-known Colombian boxer. While there Mr. T and I would slip out of the hotel and be escorted/driven to a remote, covert future landing strip so we could assess if it was suitable for the Convair 440, which was a large aircraft with forty-four seats when in passenger configuration.

We arrived in Barranquilla and as scheduled were picked up by our Colombian contacts who drove us to the remote strip. It was a six-hour drive there, most of it on four-wheel drive trails. This resulted in us staying overnight in the jungle, which was infested with mosquitoes the size of a Piper Cub and snakes. Very big snakes.

The next morning I was walking and pacing the dirt runway checking the distance we needed for landing and takeoff. You always need a lot more distance for takeoff than landing. I was about halfway down the runway when a Jeep pulls up, driven by a Colombian who said in his broken English, "Get in and take the mileage off the odometer."

Good idea. So I did that while still being eaten alive by mosquitoes and other large, blood-foraging bugs. (Tip: use Deep-Woods Off; it works best. We bought it by the case.) I reported back to Captain T that we had the necessary takeoff length needed. Or so I assumed. I later realized the odometer was calibrated for kilometers, not miles.

Oops. (Sigh)

Mr. T and I returned to the hotel, packed our bags, and boarded a flight to San Juan. Over the following days the new mission was meticulously flight planned down to the last detail and contingency. Mr. T was a true professional and an attention-to-detail kind of guy, leaving no scenario unplanned for.

Finally it was go-day! The crew was Captain T, First Officer/copilot Super Ratón, me, and our mechanic Moisase. The trip launched from San Juan International during daylight hours so we'd land in Colombia at dusk or later. The trip went as flight planed, and we arrived in Colombia just before dark.

On approach to the runway Mr. T said, "Boy, that strip sure looks short."

I pointed to the hut on the side of the runway as a landmark. "That has to be it, but you're right; it does look awfully short."

We landed and both yelled, "Holy shit, it's *too* short!"

Unbeknownst to us it had rained hard a couple of hours before we landed, so the dirt runway was now a mud pit. On landing, the main wheels touched down first, and the left gear sunk into the mud. As the nose gear touched down, it also dug into the mud. As luck would have it, the right main gear was on top of the runway. When we came to a stop, the nose gear was buried in about a foot of mud, and the left main gear was about two feet down, the mud almost reaching the gear door.

We were trapped like rats in Colombia. It was fully dark when we deplaned and were met by the chief of the local Colombian tribe. He was wearing a loincloth, sandals, and a solid gold Rolex President watch. The chief invited our crew to be his guests for dinner at his hooch. We accepted.

There were a lot of local tribesmen and women standing on the runway staring at the Convair 440 as if a spaceship had just landed in the Jungle. Right about then I heard what I could only describe as an animal death cry. All the locals ran off, and I thought the military might be approaching. The chief laughed and explained the cry was the dinner bell for the locals.

"They slaughtered a cow for their dinner in celebration of your arrival."

We arrived at the chief's compound and saw what was for our dinner. The barbecue was on, and the main course was a twelve-foot water snake roasting on a spit over the fire, with the head still on and tongue sticking out.

Well, the snake really did taste like chicken.

After dinner our crew boarded the Convair, pulled up the airstair, and closed all doors and windows for night-night. Before climbing into my sleeping bag, I looked out the cockpit windows and to my amazement saw a couple of hundred natives with candles sitting in front of the aircraft and all the way down the runway.

It looked like a rock concert without the music.

I lay down, turned on my Sony Walkman, and fell asleep to my favorite song, "The Smuggler's Blues" by Glen Frey.

It was a short but welcome rest. Very early the next morning we were awakened by the nose of the aircraft rocking up and down. Mr. T and I jumped up, immediately thinking we hadn't set the parking brake, but we saw we weren't rolling; just the nose was moving up and down. Deplaning, we saw about fifty natives had gotten under the nose and were moving it to wake us up. It worked.

While we were sleeping the natives had dug a ramp in front of the nose gear and another in front of the left main gear. Under the chief's direction they had also wrapped a four-inch thick rope around the left gear. Each rope was about one-hundred-feet long. The plan was to have a hundred natives on each rope pull while Mr. T and I ran the right engine at full power.

We gave it a go, and the rope snapped. Two hundred natives all went down like dominos.

It took about an hour to repair the rope and try again. This time I turned the water injection on as Mr. T bought the right engine to full power. It worked. We were out and free. We agreed to wait all day and let the dirt strip harden up under the blazing Colombian sun and takeoff at dusk to airdrop at night.

During the day I did another walk of the strip to determine the actual length. This was when I discovered my miscalculation on the previous visit. I approached Captain T as he was negotiating with the chief about how much product we could take and was waiting for my analysis.

I said to Mr. T, "Do you want the good news or the bad news first?"

"Give me the good news."

"There is no good news. We're about eight hundred feet short for takeoff with a full load of product."

After a brief but heated argument/negotiation during which the chief threatened to turn our aircraft into tree houses for his people, it was agreed to transport half of the product. Even at that we were over safe weight, so the takeoff would be iffy at best because we had to clear the jungle's trees at the end of the strip.

Soon enough it was go-time. We couldn't delay any longer because there were rumors swirling that Colombian Army ground forces were nearby. We had set up markers to act as airspeed points down the right side of the runway so the copilot could see them on takeoff and call them out to the captain as he controlled the plane.

For takeoff I turned on the water injection, and the blue armed light came on. Mr. T brought both Pratt & Whitney R2800 engines up to takeoff power—and then some. As we roared down the runway, I remember passing the eighty-mph marker and saw we were only doing sixty.

Thinking *this is not going to be good*, we reached the end of the usable runway. Sill low on airspeed Captain T pulled back on the yoke, and amazingly the aircraft left the ground but was climbing too slowly to miss the trees.

Now thinking *this is going to hurt* as the nose of the aircraft impacted the tops of the trees, the propellers on both engines managed to cut through the trees, and we continued our climb out. Because of the season and the rains, the trees were soft and sappy.

We had escaped death yet again.

We continued the flight to the drop area off a very small, barren island called *Cabo Muerte*, which means cape of death.

Before the takeoff from Colombia, Moisase had removed the aft left passenger door and stowed it inside, so we had an opening to jettison our cargo. We had packed the product in refrigerator-size cardboard boxes then secured them with steel bands.

That was a mistake.

When we tried to jettison the first box, it jammed halfway out the door because of the airstream hitting it. We ended up cutting that box up along with the others and throwing the product out by hand, meaning it was scattered all over the island, some even landing in trees.

On the way back to San Juan, we threw all the cut-up cardboard and banding out the door.

Mistake #2.

We didn't realize that some of the cardboard had wrapped around the left stabilizer and elevator. On short approach to the airport, the plane started to stall about one hundred feet off the ground because the cardboard was preventing aerodynamic air flow. Mr. T shoved both engines to max power, and it was enough to round out the landing.

We landed hard, and while taxiing the chunks of cardboard were falling all over the runway and taxiway. But because it was night nobody in the tower or the port authority noticed. We parked the bird and all went home.

Epilogue: The drop island was uninhabited, but it was still maintained by the National Park Service. Unbeknownst to Pepe, it had been scheduled for its annual maintenance the day after the drop. The product found all over Cabo Muerte made the front page of the local Puerto Rican newspaper. Pepe was not happy.

Lobster Stew

Mr. T and I realized the Convair-440 was too heavy for the types of landings our missions required. We agreed a DC-3 was much better suited for short dirt strips. But before switching planes, we had to take one last trip with the Convair. What could possibly go wrong, right? Ha.

We were flying from San Juan to South Caicos—also called the Big South—in the Turk and Caicos Islands. We were missing Mr. T on this trip because he was attending to some off-island business. En route we got a call on our ham radio to divert to Grand Turk because the electric generator on the fuel farm in South Caicos had failed and getting fuel there was questionable. So we landed in Grand Turk for fuel.

That was our first mistake.

While refueling we were visited by the local drug enforcement officer. He was British. Not surprising because Grand Turk is a British protectorate.

Him: Where are you guys coming from and where are you going?

Me: We're going to South Caicos.

Him: You're sure loading a lot of fuel for a thirty-minute trip.

Me: After South Caicos we're continuing on to Miami.

Him: What are all these 4'x4'x4' plywood boxes for?

Me: We're loading lobster in South Caicos to take to Miami.

Him (smiling): I see ...

Apparently I was the only person who didn't know there was no lobster in the local waters of South Caicos. Oh, well ...

We left Grand Turk for South Caicos and arrived with enough fuel to make it to Colombia. But the trip got postponed for twenty-four hours because our Colombian counterparts had been worried about fueling in South Caicos. That was just enough time for the Brit narco official to round up his strike force and assault our hotel on South Caicos.

Bummer.

We were arrested and flown back to Grand Turk for questioning. After the interrogation, which went nowhere, we were escorted to the Grand Turk Penitentiary where we were to spend the night before being deported the next day. When we arrived at the front gate of the prison, the warden was waiting for us holding a billy club.

The Brit laughed. "Oh, yes, the warden likes to beat his prisoners."

After we were all inside and the gate locked, the warden told us, "Well, boys, I've already been paid by your boss. We have a full bar here, and the girls are on the way. Try to get a good night's sleep."

We didn't. And the next day we were all deported.

My Extended Vacation

It was around the time we were expelled from Turks and Caicos that I was approached by a three-letter government agency. Obviously, they had been keeping tabs. The gist of the one-sided conversation was this:

Doctor, you're on the government's radar. You're up to six pages on the Customs data base. You need to take a permanent vacation!

So I took a two-year hiatus and got a job as a flight engineer on a Boeing 727 flying for the Saudi Royal family. The job was based in Riyadh—far, far away from Columbia. On one trip I was flying with a royal family prince to the main island in the Seychelles, which is an archipelago about nine hundred miles east of Kenya in the Indian Ocean. We landed just after the famous mercenary, Thomas Michael "Mad Mike" Hoare, had shot up the airport and escaped with his crew on an Air India Boeing 707.

Hoare was a British-Irish mercenary known for military activities in Africa, but his exploits in the Seychelles made him infamous and Exhibit A in for how not to stage a coup.

Britain foisted independence on the Seychelles in 1976. Its first president, James (call me Jimmy) Mancham has been described as an amiable playboy. While off in London having a tryst, his communist-leaning, Russian-friendly, autocratic-aspiring prime minister Albert Rene seized power. So in May 1978 a group of wealthy Seychelles residents hired Hoare to overthrow the new president and return the former president to power.

Hoare planned the coup for two years: his team of mercenaries would pose as members of a South African rugby team coming to the Seychelles on a boozy holiday. Once in country they would secure strategic areas then be joined by Kenyan forces that would toss out the usurper Rene and reinstate Mancham.

Well, even in the mercenary soldier world, good help is hard to find. Hoare's team members, who were earning $1,000 each to pull off the coup, included some special forces guys and former intelligence operatives as well as an Italian actor named Tullio Moneta, best known for his role in *The Wild Geese,* a 1978 film starring Richard Burton and Roger Moore about a group of British mercenaries hired to rescue a deposed African president from the hands of a corrupt African dictator (seriously, you can't make this stuff up). Also in the team was Sven Forsell, a former opera singer turned aspiring filmmaker who wanted to do a documentary about mercenaries. Mad Mike dubbed his team Ye

Ancient Order of Froth Blowers in homage to a posh English social club of the 1930s.

Hoare and his merry band of forty-five ragtag soldiers for hire flew into Victoria on November 25, 1980, ready for action. They never made it past Customs.

Hoare and forty-four of his men—all dressed in matching team blazers, slacks, and tote bags that carried their weapons—got in the *Nothing to Declare* line at Customs and were waved through by trusting Seychelles Customs officers. But Kevin Beck, who claimed to be a former South African intelligence officer and who had a little too much liquid courage on the flight over, was one of the last off the plane and inadvertently got in the *Something to Declare* line. When the Customs agents opened his bag and found his weapons, Beck panicked and threw his cohorts under the bus by allegedly saying: "I don't know what it is, but there are forty-four more of them in the bags outside."

When a Customs inspector ran out of the building for help, Hoare and his men armed themselves inside and took hostages. In the chaos one of the mercenaries was accidentally shot by a fellow mercenary's friendly fire, becoming the sole fatality in a plan gone horribly wrong.

Hoare and his team soon found themselves in a standoff with members of the equally ragtag Seychelles army.

Mad Mike declared himself ready to fight to the death. His men … not so much. So when an Air India Boeing 707 made a scheduled landing, the mercenaries pressured Hoare to get them out of Dodge. Hoare relented and after some negotiating, the Air India captain allowed them on board for a civilized hijacking to South Africa.

In a news report, one of the stewardesses said: "They were so polite and gentlemanly that it just did not seem as if we were being hijacked."[1]

Like I said, you can't make this stuff up. And yes, it gave me a pang of nostalgia. Because not only did you make good money as a mercenary, it was always an adventure. Maybe an adventure with moments of terror, but mostly it was grown men playing cowboys and Indians—or smugglers and DEA agents to be more exact—and instead of horses we had planes.

Many years later while frequenting my favorite watering hole, the (in)famous Palm Canyon Road House in Palm Springs, California. I met a gentleman I'll call Irish. Sharing stories over cocktails I find out he was one of Mad Mike's froth blowers.

---

[1] To read more about the coup that wasn't, check out *The Seychelles Affair* by Mad Mike Hoare

Seriously, what are the odds?

We figured out Irish was escaping on the Air India plane as I was landing in the Seychelles. I also "landed" on page 105 of Mad Mike's *The Seychelles Affair*.

Not only is it a small world, it's also a round world. As in what goes around comes around. So after my two-year hiatus, I returned to the United States to find the pilot job market saturated by post-Vietnam military flyboys. And major airlines were not hiring because of a downturn in the economy. Sooo, I made a call to the boys.

Their response was: "Doctor, come on home!"

Flashback, the DC-3

Probably not long after the first planes were built, some enterprising entrepreneur was using one for moving contraband of one sort or another. We used a variety of planes for our operations over the years, but the plane of choice was the DC-3, so named because it was the Douglas company's third model.

The DC-3 was introduced in December 1935 as a so-called sleeper transport for American Airlines. From 1936 to 1939 passenger air traffic increased fivefold and by the end of the decade, the DC-3 was carrying more than 90 percent of all domestic air passengers. During World War II, the military version of the DC-3 was the C-47, nicknamed the Gooney Bird, earned a glowing reputation for its durability and safety. According to Donnell Douglas, the twin-engine propeller plane has flown more miles, hauled more freight, and carried more passengers than any other aircraft in history.

In the 1980s they were a workhorse of a different kind; I'm guessing in its cargo configuration, it probably also smuggled more weed than any other type of aircraft in history.

When production stopped in 1946, more than ten thousand DC-3s had been built. As of 2016, it was estimated about four hundred DC-3s were still operational around the world. And one of those is mine.

As the late syndicated newspaper columnist—and big-game hunter—Robert C. Ruark waxed poetic: "They thrived on a steady diet of neglect and overwork. They flew with sand in the carburetor and were maintained by cannibals and aborigines. They rattled, banged, jumbed, and bounced, but by and large they flew."

Chapter Four: Miami Mike

Flying billionaire sheiks around was fine and all, but it was a bit formal for my tastes. It was time to go back to real work.

Smuggler's Blues 2.0, here I come!

Early on during this second go-round I was introduced to Miami Mike. Our first meeting took place at Miami's Club Pink Pussycat. Saudi Arabia may have oil coming out of its ass, but South Beach has the corner on exotic dance venues. The club was on 36th Street, conveniently located just a few blocks from Miami International.

In case the name didn't give it away, Club Pink Pussycat was a strip club favored by the drug- and gun-running pilots and boat crews. It was a meet-and-greet spot where Colombian, Panamanian, Cuban, American, and any other dark-side resident of the world could mix and talk without suspicion. The place was so entrenched that everyone used Pink Pussycat money. Literally. It was club currency printed on pink— yes, *that* shade of pink—paper with a picture of a nude woman in the center. It was called pink money and one Pink Pussycat dollar had a face value of one US dollar.

Why, you may ask, would a club have its own currency? Because it was untraceable, so it became the currency of choice for many a transaction.

In the middle of the club was a stand-alone area called the Champagne Room. It rented for $1,000. Per hour. Why, you may ask, would anyone want to spend that much money on an ugly, claustrophobic cell? Because the Champagne Room was actually built as a Faraday cage, meaning it was impenetrable by electronic eavesdroppers and also soundproof, making it the venue of choice for making deals.

Club Pink Pussycat was truly a full-service venue and was a home away from home for many years to come. So it was fitting that's where I first encountered Miami Mike, an older gentleman with a sordid past, even by mercenary standards. He'd also had his share of close calls. He used to fly some mercenary jobs until his plane crashed in the ocean leaving him injured and floating on top of an empty fuel tank while watching the surviving crew members get eaten by sharks. Taking that as a sign, he went into management and was now content to stay behind a desk. He started an aviation company at a warehouse about a mile south of the Pink Pussycat. We agreed to do some business together. I would be operating a specially equipped DC-3 nicknamed the *Millennium Falcon* out of Freeport on Grand Bahama Island.

The *Millennium Falcon* was equipped with 1,200-gallon fuel tank wings with quick-disconnect fuel bladders inside the cabin. She had an inward opening parachute door for jettisoning cargo—or personnel— and was equipped with heavy-duty landing gear. She also featured a clear, round viewing bubble/window on the top of the aircraft, and as a really nice touch, both the captain and co-pilot had rearview mirrors. The plane also had some special *de rigueur* extras all the cool kids had such as counter measures to detour unwanted government chase planes.

My check out in the plane was watching a videotape in Mike's office of a Customs Citation jet chasing the *Falcon*. The footage was narrated by Geraldo Rivera who was imbedded onboard the Customs jet at the time. The Citation had to peel off and go home because of the Falcon's counter measures—a steady stream of steel, titanium, and aluminum nuts, bolts, and rivets coming out of the bird. There were racks and racks of muffin trays full of this "ordnance" bolted to the aft bulkhead for such situations.

Next I needed a new crew. Another popular mercenary pilot hangout in Miami was the Pilot House, not far from Club Pink. If you needed a DC-6 flight engineer, you just needed to go to the Pilot House bar around closing time and ask if any flight engineer wanted some high-risk, high-reward work. We always got our man. The Pilot House was like a union hall for retired and out-of-work pilots and flight engineers.

A few weeks after rounding up a crew, it was off to Freeport, Grand Bahama. Bob, one of my old crewmates from the now-defunct DC-3 airline in Puerto Rico, would be joining me as one of my co-pilots. Bob was between corporate flying jobs and was up for some adventure and some $$$. Soon we were gearing up for our first mission.

The Plan

We'd fly from Freeport to Colombia to load product only as we had the fuel for the return trip on board already. Then fly to the drop zone in the Bahamas via flying "between" Haiti and the Dominican Republic by traveling literally above the countries' shared border to avoid provoking either's military.

The Reality

The flight to Colombia, landing, and loading were uneventful. But on the return trip things got dicey. First, between now carrying product and the extra fuel for the trip back, we were overweight on takeoff. We used US Air Force loading weights and charts for the DC-3, which assumes no engine failure on takeoff. You know what they say about assuming ...

It was dark when we were approaching Cabo Rojo. That would be our southern entry point on the Haitian-Dominican border. It was about then that the radio operator was looking out the Plexiglas bubble on the top of the aircraft and spotted what we'd later identify as the Customs Citation jet trailing us.

The boys called me the doctor of flight operations for good reason; I still had some tricks in my bag!

The first is knowing there is *always* bad weather and thunderstorms over Pétion-Ville Haiti. Basically a suburb of Port-au-Prince, Pétion-Ville is one of the highest points on Haiti and next to the boarder entrance. Sure enough, I entered a level five thunderstorm before reaching the boarder entrance, but the Customs jet peeled off in a hard-braking left turn to avoid entering the violent thunderstorm. That was the good news.

The bad news was that while flying through the intense storm, the *Millennium Falcon*'s Pratt & Whitney R-1830-92 engines were ingesting so much rainwater that the right engine sputtered out, even with full carburetor heat on. Unfortunately we had taken off from Freeport with the left engine's electrical generator inoperable.

Obviously, that had been a mistake because now we had no electrical power. The radio operator duct taped a glow stick under the flight instrument dash for illumination, but it was still hard to see; there was so much water coming through the windshield frames and the overhead escape hatch frame that it was like taking a shower with your clothes on. But after punching through the back side of the storm cell, I managed to get the right engine up and running again.

That crisis averted, it was time to get back to the mission at hand. The border between Haiti and the Dominican Republic is denoted by a river with very steep canyon walls on both sides, the distance across maybe just one hundred yards in some places. So the night procedure was for Bob to fly the *Falcon* by holding onto the steering wheel lightly, maintaining heading, altitude, and airspeed from the right seat. I was wearing first-gen night vision goggles, which turn everything green.

Sitting in the pilot's seat, with my hands resting on the steering wheel, my job was to keep the left wing away from the canyon wall. A real-life video game with real-life consequences.

Once down in the winding canyon at night, usually with a weather cap above us, it was next to imposable to follow us. This escape route exits at Cap-Haïtien—usually just called Le Cap—the most northern point on Haiti. We turned left and staying low flew to our drop point in the Bahamas, where forty to sixty feet long, open deck cigarette boats waited. Usually operated by the famous Blue Dolphin gang, these cigarette racers were equipped with four, 200 hp Black Max Mercury outboard motors on a hydraulically adjustable tube frame and when fully loaded with product, could run at top speed in just thirty-seven inches of water. I should point out Coast Guard ships could not. So the cigarette boats worked great, until the Coast Guard and DEA got helicopters out there.

Flash forward: Years later while flying as a DC-8 captain for a legit cargo airline, I was in the break room of our main hub where the flight crews congregated between trips. I was talking to some crewmembers when a new co-pilot named Mike walked up.

"Excuse me; but I overheard some crewmembers calling you the Doctor."

"Yeah …"

"I used to fly the Customs Citation jet."

Like I said, it's a small pilot world. Mike was a former F-16 military pilot and explained the Citation had the F-16 radar as well as GPS and forward-looking infrared radar (FLIR).

"One night I was over Cabo Rojo following a DC-3 with the right engine out," Mike said. "It went into a level five thunderstorm and never came out. We lost it." Wait for it … "Was that you?"

I looked at Mike. "Was that you with the wing strobe lights that made the breaking left turn out?"

We both laughed then left on our respective trips.

#

While we operated from Freeport, Miami Mike rented a large, five-bedroom home on the island. Known as the safe house, one bedroom was used as a radio and operations room, two for the flight crew, and two for our A-team, which was usually five to eight ex-special forces guys hired as security on and off the mission.

It was at the safe house at 2:00 a.m. where I meet the truly famous and infamous number one mercenary pilot, Chung, so called because he was Chinese. (Nobody ever claimed mercenaries were politically correct). Over the years I had moved up from number five to number two, more from attrition than derring-do. The previous second-rated pilot killed himself impacting that mountain in Haiti and the number three and four pilots were in a Colombian prison.

I had no illusions of ever being number one because Chung was the undisputed champion and for good reason. He was certifiable.

The Load

The Freeport safe house was out in the countryside not far from the beach. As I was in the kitchen reaching for another Beck's beer, I saw an elderly Chinese man with white hair and Coke-bottle glasses banging on the sliding glass door to the backyard.

Mike was visiting, and I yelled out to him, "Hey, your gardener's outside banging on the door to the backyard."

Confused, Mike walked into the kitchen and looked toward the door. "Ho-ly shit; it's Chung!"

Mike quickly opened the door, and they both rushed into the radio room, Chung excited and speaking half broken English and half Chinese. About five to ten minutes later they reappeared and rounded up our A-team.

As everyone was leaving for the airport I asked Mike, "Wuz up?"

"Chung has just landed an overweight DC-3 with product at the airport."

That Mike, such a jokester. "No way; the Feds would have captured him and his crew before the wheels stopped turning."

Mike was dead serious. "He feathered both engines and dead-sticked the DC-3 on the runway." Meaning he had shut down the power in the air and landed with no power so nobody could hear or see the plane.

The only response I could think of as Mike, Chung, and the crew left to recover the product was: "*Bullshit!* I'm going to bed."

I woke up around ten or eleven the next morning. As I popped my breakfast beer, I looked out the kitchen window onto the backyard where an enormous blue plastic tarp covered 110 fifty- to fifty-seven-pound bales of product. I immediately jumped on the house moped and rode to the airport. To my utter amazement there was the DC-3 sitting sideways off the end of the runway with both engines feathered and Feds crawling all over it.

Turns out Chung's father was a Chinese Air Force General. He started flying DC-3s with his father as a small boy. Later in life and before the mercenary flying, Chung flew U-2 spy planes over Red China—on loan from you know what alphabet agency—for General Chiang Kai-Shek. Chung had amassed twenty thousand flight hours in DC-3s by the time of our meeting.

And that's why I never made it to number one.

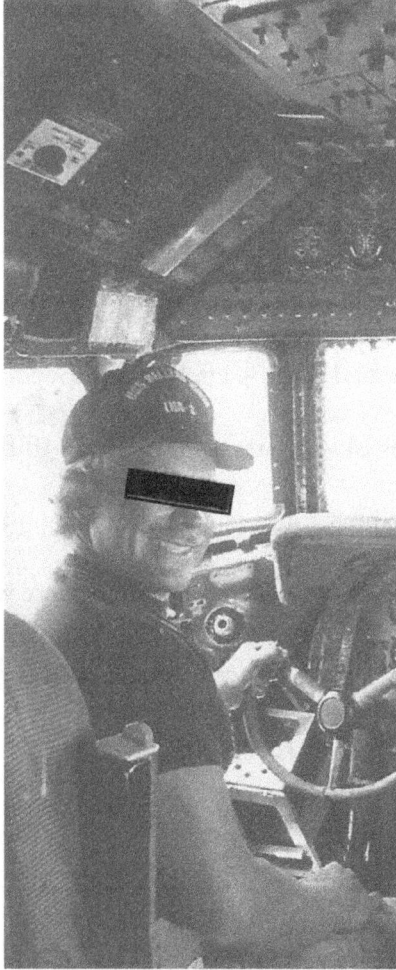

In the cockpit of our DC-6

Flashback, Pirates of the Caribbean

There are times when the light is right, the wind rustling through the palm trees, and enough beer has been consumed that you can imagine what the Bahamas were like back in the pirates' heyday. Several famous pirates did plenty of their treasure hunting and pillaging on and around the islands we modern-day aerial privateers were in the game. One was Calico Jack, who was romantically involved with another pirate legend, Anne Bonny.

Because Great Inagua is the third largest island in the Bahamas, it had its fair share of pirate visits so its history is woven with many legends of buried treasure. According to one, a treacherous Haitian King buried treasure on Great Inagua in the 1800s, somewhere near the island's northeast point, but so far that treasure has never been found.

A lot of pirates were more scavengers than masterminds. Shipwrecks occurred constantly, so they'd hang around the outskirts of the island waiting for ships to crack a hull on some of the reefs or run aground on an unexpected sandbar. Once the ship was inoperable or sinking, plundering was easy pickings. Island folk like to believe the pirates hid their loot and treasures in any one of the island's numerous coves, but I never heard of anyone ever finding any gold or booty on Inagua or anywhere else.

The pirates of yore were more of an organized bunch than you would expect. They founded the Republic of Pirates in Nassau on New Providence island as a base of operations, complete with a governor and an informal code of conduct. The republic—which was more hangout than sovereign state—operated from 1706 until 1718 until the British showed up and sent them packing.

The era of piracy in the Bahamas had begun in earnest in 1696 when Henry Every sailed into Nassau harbor. His ship, the Fancy, was loaded with loot "appropriated" from Indian trade vessels. In true pirate fashion, Henry bribed the island's governor, officially establishing Nassau as a safe harbor where pirates could operate safely. Oh, sure, various governors periodically made a show of suppressing piracy while pocketing the bribes and keeping the pirates one step ahead of the British and French.

Sound familiar? The vessels, cargo, and centuries might change, but pirate or mercenary, the way of doing outlaw business doesn't.

Chapter Five: Captain Nemo's Island

After the Chung affair the US Feds, the Bahamian Defence Force, and the islands' Criminal Investigation Division (CID) dramatically beefed up their presence on Grand Bahama. So much so it forced us rats to leave the sinking Freeport ship. Miami Mike moved the operation east to Great Inagua, the Bahamas's southernmost island, located just fifty-five miles from the eastern tip of Cuba as the crow flies. Before we showed up the biggest attraction on Great Inagua—which we called Captain Nemo's Island—was its famous pink flamingo breeding ground. The Inagua National Park is home to more than eighty thousand birds. The island is home to less than one thousand people.

The Great Inagua airport was located in Matthew Town, which was little more than a poor fishing village with dirt roads. There was no doctor or medical facility on the island, and air service was sporadic, maybe one flight a week in and out. There was zero infrastructure in place at the time to support our operation, so we built it.

The first project was a simple, four-room motel for us crew. Since we didn't want anything to be traced back to us, we literally gave the building to a local elderly couple. In exchange for us giving them a deed, they agreed to run it as a motel and keep the rent. The one rule/request was that whenever our crew arrived to stay, there could be no other guests. We gave them plenty of notice, usually two weeks, so that was never an issue.

The second project was the bar. Pirates always need a safe place to drink. We built the bar with a kitchen to serve meals. We then brought thousands of pounds of booze, food, and entertainment equipment in on the DC-3. When the bar was finished, we gave it to a young, entrepreneurial Bahamian man who was the town mover and shaker.

The one rule/request for him was that we were all to remain anonymous, our true identities protected. He happily complied.

This was a dirt poor community, so we shared the wealth and cared for the people, like when we brought in four brand-new tires for the local Customs lady's car. Then a week before Thanksgiving our crew was leaving on our boss's turbine Aero Commander to pick up the DC-3 in Miami and ferry it back to Great Inagua. While walking through Matthew Town the night before. I had overheard some locals talking about how they wouldn't have enough food to feed everyone at the church's Thanksgiving dinner—yes, many people celebrate Thanksgiving in the Bahamas. Who knew?

When I got to Miami I mentioned to Mike how the church was sponsoring Thanksgiving dinner for all the locals but wouldn't have enough food. A couple of days later when the flight crew and I boarded the DC-3 for the trip back to Great Inagua, we found it packed to the max with cases of frozen turkeys on ice along with cases and cases of canned goods.

The church provided a lavish Thanksgiving dinner for literally all the locals. And we were invited too.

#

We flew many trips from Captain Nemo's Island, and it didn't go unnoticed. The US Coast Guard was now flying their Falcon jet over the runway at Matthew Town every morning. And I'm assuming they were taking pictures of the airport ramp and DC-3 to see if it had moved.

So we devised a plan to make the DC-3 look like a derelict aircraft off the side of the runway.

We decowled the right engine, feathered the right propeller, and deflated the right main landing gear tire. We also sprayed rust colored splotches on the top of the wing. It worked. Then at night we would pump up the right tire using the aircraft's engine as an air compressor and an air hose fitting I made that screwed into the engine cylinder. We would then re-cowl the right engine, unfeather the propeller, and we were good to go. On our return we would just reverse the process and roll the aircraft back in its original tracks.

One morning I came to the bar for some breakfast. Some locals were there, and they all seemed very depressed, so I asked what was up. They explained that one of the local young men had been welding his car's gas tank, and it blew up. Although he had removed the gas, he didn't purge the tank. He was badly burned and needed immediate emergency medical treatment, but as I said, there was no doctor on the island, so his prognosis was grim.

Our boss's Aero Commander was about to leave for Miami, so I talked the pilot into medivacing the young man to the main hospital in Nassau on New Providence Island before continuing on to Miami. The boss's pilot was Ecuadorian, a talented pilot, and also a great guy. He agreed.

The pilot returned unexpectedly the next day. I greeted him when he walked into the bar and asked why he was back. He had spent the night at the hospital in Nassau trying to convince US government authorities to allow the young Bahamian to enter the country without a passport because doctors in Nassau said he needed to be transported to the

Grady Burn Center in Atlanta, Georgia, because his condition was beyond the capabilities of the small island hospital.

The response from the US authorities was no passport, no entry.

It was complete bullshit, and I was pissed. I told the boss's pilot, who had been up and flying all night, to load up one of his relatives with a Bahamian passport, and I'd fly the Aero Commander to Nassau, pick the patient up, and transport him to the burn center in Atlanta.

The boss's pilot reminded me that I had a trip the next day, so he did it and successfully got the young Bahamian to Atlanta. That pilot was a real hero. But too much time had passed, and the young man died. I cursed the inhumane governmental bureaucracy that valued policy over humanity and compassion.

A couple of weeks later a corporate jet landed at Matthew Town. It was around noon, and I was the only one in the bar when an older, dignified Bahamian gentleman with white hair walked in and sat down at the other end of the bar. He was very well-dressed in a powder-blue leisure suit with matching white corfam belt and shoes.

He said, "I'm looking for the Doctor."

Of course I said, "I've never heard of him."

He smiled at me. "Well, should you see him, please tell him he no longer has an immigration problem anywhere in the Bahamas."

As he was walking out of the bar, I asked, "Who are you?"

He stopped and turned to face me. "I'm the head minister of immigration for the Bahamas, and that young Bahamian man *you* had transported to the burn center was my nephew."

Then he left.

#

Despite our subterfuge with the DC-3, things were heating up on Great Inagua, so sadly it was time to abandon Captain Nemo's Island. Specifically, the Feds assaulted the island, and we had to scram. The *Millennium Falcon* was also a casualty.

The day before the raid my old copilot, Al the Super Ratón, and I had tried to relocate the DC-3. But unbeknownst to us, while our crew was off island, Miami Mike had subbed out our DC-3 to another crew for a trip. When they returned they ground looped the aircraft when landing, meaning the pilot allowed the tail to swing out too far, causing the plane to tip and drag a wing along the ground, damaging the left aircraft elevator. The elevators are the control surfaces on an airplane that make the aircraft pitch nose up or down, which enables the plane to rise or descend. You can't fly without properly working elevators. So the problem was supposedly fixed.

On the day of our planned relocation, I preflighted the outside of the DC-3 while the Super Ratón prepped the cockpit from the right seat. Everything looked in order. We were fully loaded with 1,200 gallons of fuel in the wings and another two hundred gallons in a fuel bladder in the cargo cabin. The DC-3 burned one hundred gallons per hour so we had fourteen hours of flight time.

After our preflight and run up checks were complete, I made the takeoff. To my surprise as I climbed out the aircraft started a left turn on its own. It took both the Super Ratón and me on the control wheels to handle it. Having no choice, we made a left circuit and managed to land the DC-3 back on the Great Inagua runway.

We later learned that when the aircraft was repaired before our crew returned to the island, whoever worked on it had rigged the left elevator trim tab upside down. Definitely *no bueno*. We were lucky to get back on the ground in one piece.

And there went yet another of my rapidly decreasing nine lives.

The Bimini Trip

Not a lot of people can instantly recall the worst day or days of their life. I can. It all started with the flight planning meeting in the Champagne Room of the Pink Pussy Cat.

Miami Mike had lined up a super high-risk but high-reward trip that entailed flying a really old Piper Aztec light twin-engine aircraft of the 1960's vintage, which even then was considered almost prehistoric. It was white with red stripe accents.

Our mission, if we chose to accept it—and of course we did—was to launch from Bimini Island in the Bahamas, fly to Boscobel, Jamaica, pick up a load of Jamaican red, airdrop it to cigarette boats waiting south of Bimini, then return to the island.

I might have been thinking: *Not so fast, cowboy!* But I ultimately went along with the plan. And my darkest days started when I landed on Bimini Island with only the two front seats installed and a whole lot of cargo space behind them.

Bimini's biggest claim to fame was supposedly being Ernest Hemingway's favorite escape, and back then the main street was still a dirt road. The island is only fifty miles off the Florida coast, so my arrival was noticed. The plane had barely rolled to a stop when I was immediately greeted by Bimini's chief of police—not as impressive of a title as you may think. Being a very small island, the police force consisted of the chief and his deputy, Sergeant Dean. That was it.

The chief looked like Mr. T from the *A-Team* television series, except I think the chief was bigger. And he was not happy to see me. He wasn't much for conversation and got to the point.

He said, and I quote, "If you're doing what I think you're doing here, you won't make it to jail. I'll feed you to the sharks."

Turns out my old pal Triple X had arrived on the island before me. He was flying as copilot on a Citation privet charter jet. And the captain was an old and trusted friend of mine, Mr. MT. I ran into them at the Bimini Big Game Bar & Grill Restaurant on the waterfront, which at the time was the only restaurant around.

As I explained the plan to my friends, MT stopped me. "Doctor, do you know how to start a Citation jet?"

"No."

So the next day MT schooled me on how to start, fly, and operate the Citation in case I needed it as an escape pod off the island. It was both comforting and not.

MT was/is a man's man, an ex-Vietnam long-range reconnaissance patrol guy who could still *kick ass!* The day before my ill-fated trip, Triple

X, MT, and I had cocktails at the (in)famous End of the World Bar in Bimini. I was assigned a copilot who wasn't a pilot. He was an overweight Cuban who didn't speak any English, and my Spanish was still weak, to say the least.

The flight left as planned. So far so good. At least for the first five minutes. Then things started going wrong. I discovered that while in the Champaign Room at the Pink Pussy Cat, during the flight planning phase, Miami Mike had given me the wrong coordinates for Boscobel, so I landed at the wrong airport in Jamaica.

Yeah, big oops.

We were meet by the local airport police with, "What you doing here, mon?"

I gave them $400, and they said Boscobel was five miles north. Good to know. So we took off for and headed for the correct airport. Apparently bribe etiquette was lost on those officers because they alerted the Jamaican Army about our planned arrival in Boscobel.

We landed and as fuel and product were being loaded, the Jamaican Army showed up, guns blazing. Under a hail of military gunfire we managed to take off, but without enough fuel to follow the original flight plan, which was to fly from Boscobel over my usual route between Haiti and the Dominican Republic then on to the drop zone before heading back to Bimini Island.

The lack of fuel limited my options to flying through the Windward Passage, a strait between the easternmost region of Cuba and the northwest of Haiti. As I said, I had no choice, but it was still a *big* mistake. The DEA and Customs, in concert with the US military, had a radar balloon, part of the Tethered Aerostat Radar System (TARS) attached to a ship east of Cuba.

What is that? you may wonder. According to the Customs and Border Patrol program manager for TARS, "The aerostats are aerodynamic balloons and fly like kites in the wind—no one pilots them. Raising radar and other sensors to high altitude boosts the surveillance range, and the physical sight of an aerostat is a visual deterrent to illegal activity in the air and on the ground. Each TARS balloon contains a radar capable of detecting aircraft at a range of two hundred miles."

So what, you may wonder, *did that mean exactly?*

Exactly, it meant I was so busted.

Not long after, I had a US Customs Citation jet trailing me from below and behind, as usual. But my day was about to get even worse as two Customs/DEA strike force Beechcraft King Air 200s, based at

Homestead Air Reserve Base in Florida, joined up on my left and right wing tips with about ten feet of separation.

By now I was nearing the drop zone and *very* low on fuel because I had been playing cat and mouse with the two King Airs, which were about one hundred knots faster than the old Aztec I was flying. Just as it was looking like I might pull it off, two new arrivals showed up. A DEA confiscated Beechcraft Queen Air that took a position above me and a Bell Huey helicopter gunship that was under me. The Huey was painted military green with *POLICE* emblazoned on the side in huge, white letters and was fitted with M-60 machineguns on both left and right door openings. And the worst part of my day was still yet to come.

At that point I climbed to 2,500 feet and jettisoned the cargo while flying a zigzag course. Since the product was only designed to survive a drop from oh, say, one hundred feet, it exploded on impact and sank. I bet there were some mellow fish in the seas that night.

The DEA-operated Queen Air and the Huey peeled off in search of the jettisoned cargo. Now it was just the two strike force King Airs and me. Around the time I was thinking: *The Doctor has a chance*, the right engine ran out of fuel. I turned on the fuel tank cross-feed switch and got the right engine back online. But it was a short-lived relief. Four minutes later the fuel tanks were empty, and both engines quit.

The propellers on the Aztec were windmilling, and the King Airs were slowing down to stay with me by putting out their flaps and lowering their landing gear. I feathered both engine propellers on the Aztec, giving me a better glide ratio. The expressions on the faces of the strike force pilots were priceless as we all saluted each other.

I was descending about two hundred feet per minute, but I had Bimini Island in view. It was about a mile in front and below us, and it looked like I could make it. The Bimini runway was at a 90-degree angle from our present heading, meaning I would have to make a hard banking left turn and blow the landing gear down with the emergency system just before landing.

Did I mention that the old Aztec aircraft did not have an emergency exit, only the main cabin door?

In my best Spanish, which wasn't saying much and clearly wasn't nearly good enough, I tried explaining to my Cuban copilot that if I couldn't make the turn to the runway, I would land in the water just off the beach and instructed him to pop the cabin door open just before landing. Well, the knucklehead goes right to the cabin door and opens it.

And then we can't close it back up. Now the aircraft is descending seven hundred feet per minute, and any hope of making it to Bimini is gone.

We're going swimming!

Finally, something went right. I managed to make a picture-perfect water landing when ditching in the ocean. By that point I was grateful for any small favors. The plane touched down about a half a mile south of Bimini, around the Orange Key area. Since the cabin door was already open—thank you, knucklehead—the aircraft quickly filled with ocean water and was sinking *fast*. I still had my seatbelt on, and looking out the windshield I saw my passport float by and realized I was underwater!

The Cuban had already exited the aircraft with the five-man life raft in a one-foot by one-foot package. As I climbed out onto the right wing to join the Cuban, the aircraft sank beneath us. We inflated the round life raft and jumped in. On impact I had broken my nose on the yoke (steering handles), and the yoke on the Cuban's side had punched a hole in his forehead. So we were both bleeding, and the bottom of the raft was covered in blood.

And now the real fun was about to start.

The two strike force King Airs were circling overhead, and it wasn't long before the Huey gunship showed up. It looked like there were two pilots wearing white helmets and dark visors. The crew chief wore a white helmet and an orange visor. Then there were another five or so armed Royal Bahamas Defence Force soldiers on board. Yikes.

The helicopter crew chief tossed out a four-pronged grappling hook made out of rebar that was attached to a yellow nylon rope. The Huey proceeded to drag the rope and grappling hook over the life raft, intending to snag it and drag us to shore. The first two times the hook landed in the raft, I threw it overboard. Then the helicopter came down and hovered just a few feet above us to try a third time. But the downdraft from its rotor blades turned the life raft inside out.

The helicopter moved off but was still hovering close by. The crew chief was holding the grappling hook. He gestured to the hook and then the M-60 machinegun in the door as if to say: *It's either the hook or the gun.*

I gave him the well-known international hand signal: the finger.

The helicopter peeled off to deposit some soldiers on the Bimini shore before leaving. After paddling for a few hours, we were only about a quarter of a mile from Bimini. All the other aircraft were also gone, and it was getting dark. *Looking good for the Doctor,* you think, right?

Ha.

Just then a Bimini police boat pulled up with none other than the police chief and his deputy, Sergeant Dean, badge #728. Needless to say the chief was not amused to see us.

After boarding the police boat at gunpoint—they were carrying FN FAL rifles—the chief proceeded to chop up the life raft with a machete and threw the remnants in the back of the boat. Then he asked me where the plane was. It was now dark, and I could see the radio beacon on Bimini Island (frequency 396, I believe). I could also see the boat's compass and knew the plane was behind us. But on principle I told the chief it was in front of us.

It was a day with a long series of unfortunate events. Unfortunately, right about then the village fishing fleet found the wreck and called it into the police boat. The aircraft had lodged on a coral reef and as the tide went down the tip of the Aztec's tail was visible out of the water.

Bummer.

The chief turned around punched me in the face and threw both the Cuban and me into the ship's anchor hold then we were transported to the scene of the crime. By then the tide was back up, and the aircraft was on the white, sandy bottom. There were some American sport fishing boats at the scene with their bottom lights on, illuminating the Aztec.

Go Directly to Jail; Do Not Pass Go and Collect $200

There was no jail cell at the small, one-room police station, so the Cuban and I were seated in the middle of the room, no handcuffs. They had guns, after all. The police chief went home leaving the sergeant in charge.

A little while later M "Big Balls" T walked into the police station and announced right in front of Sergeant Dean, "Doctor, I will blow you out of here tonight!"

I laughed and said, "I got this."

After MT left I slipped Sergeant Dean a $100 bill and told him to get us a case of Heineken beer.

The sergeant said, "This is a police station."

"You know who I am?"

He nodded. "Ya, you the Doctor."

"Yes, but I'm also your genie, and if you bring back the beer, you can have one wish."

He got the case of beer then I said, "Okay, what do you want?"

Usually it was things like a big screen TV, an ATV, etc.

The Sergeant said, "I want that new Michal Jackson cassette tape, *Thriller.*"

The *Thriller* album had just been released and was sold out on the island.

My face was really swollen up and hurting, so the last thing I wanted to do was laugh. But it was hard not to.

The next morning Triple X and MT left the island. The police chief walked into the station that morning, and I could tell he was upset about something because he couldn't look me in the eye while talking. Then the station phone rang, and the chief answered it. The conversation was brief. When he hung up, he said a US government agency was sending a Blackhawk helicopter from Homestead Air Reserve Base to pick up the Cuban and me and take us to Florida.

"It will be here in forty-five minutes." The chief then looked straight at me. "You won't be here, will you?"

I said, "Not if you say we won't!"

The chief informed me, "There was not a t'ing on the aircraft; I cannot hold you."

So the Cuban and I bolted. The Cuban jumped on a fishing boat and was gone. *So long, knucklehead.*

Since I had time and no way off the island yet, I walked back into the police station and confronted the chief. "Why the change of heart?"

He looked at me. "I found out you were the one who arranged to medivac that young Bahamian man out of Great Inagua. He was my brother."

That one event was the gift that kept on giving. But I still needed to be gone because by then the Blackhawk from Homestead was less than thirty minutes out. Bimini is very small with nowhere to hide out, so I had to get off the island fast. Walking toward the beach, I considered swimming to one of the outlying reefs and make like a sea urchin. I then realized my black polo shirt was still soaked in blood, which would have made me live barracuda and shark bait.

It was then that a Chalk's International Airlines plane landed out on the surf and pulled up on the beach. Chalk's started in Miami and provided air service to some of the Bahamian Islands. They operated Grumman Turbine Mallard amphibious planes that held eighteen passengers and two crewmembers. Chalk's was even featured on the TV show *Miami Vice* and in the final scenes of the movie *Silence of the Lambs* when Dr. Frederick Chiton is seen disembarking a Chalk's aircraft in Bimini, where Hannibal Lecter is waiting to have him for dinner.

Chalk's was sold in 1996 and renamed Pan Am Air Bridge, which filed for bankruptcy three years later. A former Eastern Airlines pilot bought the company out of bankruptcy and relaunched it as Chalk's Ocean Airways. But the company shut down around December 2005 after one of their planes was involved in a fatal accident. The right wing separated from the aircraft after takeoff, and all eighteen passengers and two crew members died.

But on that day in the early 1980s, a Chalk's plane was going to be my salvation. I was now close by the Mallard. While hiding behind a palm tree planning my appropriation of the seaplane, I spotted the Chalk's captain. He had spotted me too and walked toward me. It was Nelson, an old friend from the days of operating out of San Juan, Puerto Rico. Years before I had saved Nelson's bacon when he was covertly operating an old Twin Beechcraft from the shady side of San Juan International. When the Feds decided to stake out his plane and arrest Nelson, I called and warned him. Nobody had seen him since, until that day on Bimini.

Nelson was a tall, very, very thin Puerto Rican who rarely smiled. He was wearing cheap, dark sunglasses, sported a *Miami Vice* three-day beard, and was smoking an Antonio Cleopatra cigar.

Nelson also hated gringos.

As Captain Nelson approached me, he laughed—for probably the first time in his life—and said with his heavy Spanish accent, "Well, Doctor, it looks like you need a ride out a town."

With my face still swollen and bruised, my shirt covered in dried blood, I said, "Ya think?"

He was still smiling. "Go get in the cockpit jump seat before we load passengers for Miami." Considering my appearance, Nelson also suggested I not look at the copilot and scare her.

The jump seat was between the captain and the copilot seats. Nelson and I were both in our seats while the copilot finished boarding the passengers. Then she sat in the right-side cockpit seat. I was pretending to be asleep facing Nelson in the left seat. On takeoff from Bimini Nelson made a left turn that took the seaplane over the now underwater Aztec. I looked out Nelson's window at the scene of the crime. That was probably only the second time Nelson had ever smiled.

Nelson was still smoking his cigar as we leveled out and headed for South Miami Beach where Chalk's had their base of operations.

About then the copilot said to Captain Nelson, "Did you hear that the Bahamian Defence Force shot that Aztec down, and the pilot escaped and is probably armed and dangerous."

See, this is how rumors start …

Nelson took a *looong* drag on his cigar. "Yep."

"I wonder how he got off the island."

I couldn't take it any longer. I turned around and looked directly at her with the best pirate face I could muster. She turned the color of a white sheet and froze, probably thinking the aircraft was being hijacked, eliciting a third smile from Nelson.

It was a short flight to Miami, and to my wonderment Nelson had flown to the city's North Beach instead of South Beach where the Chalk's terminal was. He then made a left turn down the Intercoastal Waterway.

The copilot was confused. "What are you doing, Captain Nelson?"

"I'm showing the passengers North Beach on the way back to base." Then he turned to me. "Doctor, do you still stay at the Fontainebleau Hotel in South Beach?"

"I do."

Nelson then transitioned the aircraft form the Intercoastal Waterway to the Atlantic Ocean side of South Beach and descended to about five feet above the water as we approached the Fontainebleau.

He then says to the copilot, "It looks like I have to shut down the right engine for low oil pressure."

Her confusion returned. "I don't see anything wrong with the right engine oil pressure."

Nelson feathers the right engine. "Do ya see it now?"

One more smile from Nelson! *Stop, you're going to hurt yourself.*

Nelson landed the Mallard in the water about fifty yards from the beach in front of the Fontainebleau. Cigar clenched between his molars, he opened the cockpit overhead escape hatch and said, "Doctor, we are now even."

It was 9:00 a.m. when I ran down the top of the Mallard's right wing and dove into the ocean wearing a black polo shirt, shorts, and tennis shoes. It was a short enough swim—back in the day when I was in great shape—but the tide was against me, and I was having a hard time making progress. I thought: *After all this drama, I'm going to drown in South Beach.*

There was no lifeguard on the beach that time of the morning for a rescue, so I had to tough it out. Miraculously I made it. As I walked out of the surf in my clothes, barefoot—I had jettisoned the tennis shoes trying not to drown—some tourist walked up and said, "Where did you come from?"

I turned around and saw there were no boats on the water. I turned back and said, "Plane crash," and kept walking to the beach entrance of the Fontainebleau. When I walked into the hotel lobby soaking wet, the concierge was the first to see me. He came running over, smiling wide.

"Doctor, how nice to see you again." Yes, I stayed there *a lot*. "The penthouse is available right this way," and he ushered me into the elevator. When we got to the penthouse, he said, "Get some sleep. We'll send up some dry clothes and a case of Crystal champagne."

As I said, I stayed there a lot.

I slept for about ten hours, and when I woke up the bed was soaked with sweat because I had relived my misadventure in my dreams.

And that, my friends, was my worst day—well, except for when I was in the Haitian National Prison. But that's a later story.

Postscript

A few days later I FedExed a *Thriller* cassette tape to Sergeant Dean, which is why I still remember his badge number to this day.

Also, around that time Miami Mike's daughter had convinced him to retire. So he did. And I was on to the next chapter.

Flashback, the Mid-1980s

Ronald Reagan's belief that communism anywhere threatened democracy everywhere—and his unreported, advancing dementia—would sow the seeds for a White House administration rife with ideologues where illegal black ops designed to further unsanctioned military and political objectives thrived.

The Iran-Iraq war began after Saddam Hussein ordered his forces to invade Western Iran. The conflict would last most of the decade, causing more than one million military and civilian casualties. Over that time it would also serve as the catalyst for a lot of alphabet-agency covert activity that kept many mercenary pilots busy and rolling in the green.

Back in Nicaragua, the US-backed rebel Contras were guided by a certain infamous Marine Lieutenant-Colonel I'll call Colonel N. The Sandinistas, a socialist political party that had ruled the country since 1979, were supported by a certain infamous cartel in Medellin, Colombia, led by the kingpin himself, El Jefe, also called Patron.

While history books classify the Contra-Sandinista conflict as a civil war, a lot more was at stake than democracy. It was ground zero for the battle over who would control the Central American drug trade. I know this first-hand because I worked as a pilot for both sides.

Yes, things were getting more complicated and riskier. It was like 3-D chess, except played with real weapons, and the rest of my nine lives were feeling the heat.

Chapter Six: The Contra-Sandinista War

We had moved our base of operations to Cap-Haïtien, a town on the most northerly point on Haiti. We called our base the Rats' Nest because the local Haitians had eaten all the cats, so the rodent population was *out of control.* There were signs all over Cap-Haïtien begging the locals to stop eating the cats. South Beach this was not.

We were in need of a new flying pirate ship and learned that our old DC-3 was impounded by the Turks and Caicos government on South Caicos Island.

If you're thinking: *Ah, payback time* ... roger that!

It wasn't long before a full-blown rescue mission was launched to retrieve the old bird. The DC-3s we used were built in 1942. They had been used in World War II and smuggling operations for the last forty years. She belonged back with us.

The Plan

My old copilot, Bob, and I would stealthily arrive on South Caicos Island posing as sports fishermen. We would then liberate our old DC-3 friend from the bonds of our old adversary, the Turks and Caicos government.

Bob and I arrived on South Caicos undetected. Years earlier when operating out of the island, I had befriended one of the local hotel owners.

Bob and I stayed at that hotel under his protection and watchful eye. It was a very small hotel with fewer than ten rooms. The owner was Hungarian, so the restaurant at the hotel was Hungarian.

That night while dining I asked the owner, "Why do you only serve Hungarian food here?"

"Because the locals *hate* Hungarian food."

During dinner one of the other hotel guests eating there, an obese Puerto Rican, waddled over to our table.

"I know you guys from somewhere," he said to us. "I just can't remember from where."

With straight faces we assured him we didn't know each other. But both Bob and I immediately recognized him. His nickname was Teke-Taka. Years earlier he was based out of the shady side of the ramp at San Juan International. He had flown a trip to Colombia, and the story I got was that he crashed on takeoff while loaded with product and had spent several years in a Colombian prison. When he returned to Puerto Rico, he went to work as an undercover narco agent.

Worried that Teke-Taka may recover his memory at any time, Bob and I decided to make our move right away. We informed our friendly hotel owner of our plan, just in case. We would get into position that night and then take off at first light.

The hotel owner said, "Just fly over the hotel on takeoff so I know you made it out."

Bob and I belly crawled a good one hundred yards across the airport grounds to get into the DC-3. There was some airport security close by in a guard shack, but we went unnoticed because they weren't expecting any activity and were distracted. Finally at first light Bob and I cranked the DC-3's engines; thank God they started right away. The aircraft wasn't chained or tied down, so we quickly powered out of the parking spot as the guards came running out of the shack.

Keeping our promise, we buzzed the hotel. But the owner later lamented that we cleared the roof by only twenty feet. He also told us that when Teke-Taka heard the roaring engines of the DC-3 overhead, he came running out of his room that early morning, half-naked, screaming: "I know those *ratóns!*"

Too late now …

Having limited fuel, Bob and I flew the DC-3 to Freeport, Grand Bahamas. Another mistake. We picked up the now familiar Customs

Citation jet along the way with the strike force's King Airs and helicopter gunships in tow.

We landed in Freeport to a rock star reception; it seemed that just about every US and Bahamian government agency were waiting for us. And they all wanted their pound of flesh. The aircraft was impounded—again—and we were arrested. After a night in jail sleeping on a hard, cold concrete floor, we were arraigned at the local court in Freeport and charged with possession of narcotics.

What?

The court date was set, and Bob and I were released to return the following month to stand trial for possession of narcotics, which we did. The Criminal Investigation Division (CID) in Freeport claimed to have found marijuana seeds in the aircraft.

Bob and I hired Mr. Tines, the best attorney money could buy. And it was all about money in those days; *everyone* had their hand out. Mr. Tines was Bahamian and the most famous attorney in the islands. He was connected to all the judges in the Bahamas, and they all trusted him.

Mr. Tines arrived at our hotel, and when he entered our room, he saw that I had laid out $100,000 US in cash on my bed. I asked Mr. Tines how much would it cost for Bob and me to be found not guilty *and* to have the DC-3 released in my name?

The answer from Mr. Tines was $15,500. I asked him why such an exacting amount?

He explained, "There is a used Mercedes on the local car lot, and the judge would like to pick it up tomorrow."

The judge ruled in our favor. The case was dismissed, and the aircraft was released in my name as captain. A celebration was in order. However, by then our new employer owed Bob and me six figures and refused to pay up.

I told him, "If you don't pay us, I'm selling the aircraft to the highest bidder."

He didn't, so I did sell the DC-3 for five figures, to be delivered anywhere in the Southern Hemisphere. The DC-3 was vandalized, I suspect by the local Feds. They had broken all the flight instruments with a ball peen hammer and ripped out all the navigation and communication radios.

But that didn't stop the Doctor.

I left with the DC-3 in that condition with the new owner—who was not a pilot—in the right seat. Our destination was San Salvador, an island in the Bahamas. As we had no flight instruments or radios, I navigated by dead reckoning, which meant looking out the window and comparing the landmarks—in this case, the islands—to our map. Miraculously I found the island. We landed, and as I depressed the brake pedals, a fitting on the hydraulic reservoir failed. We lost all the hydraulic fluid that operates the brakes, so before long all the brakes failed. We went off the end of the runway and ended up parked among the jungle trees. I had taken out a tree with the left wing, and the left main gear tire was flat. But the aircraft was delivered.

Mission accomplished, and with my remaining lives intact.

But not all us cowboys were always so lucky. Barry Seal became a well-known cautionary tale on how not to conduct your business.

The Barry Seal Affair

Most mercenary pilots fly under the radar—literally and figuratively—as much as possible. It's better for their longevity and helps keeps them out of jail. They're known to a select group of people who have need for their unique skill-sets and services, and they work with a trusted circle of compadres. Their operations are risky, but it's usually a carefully calculated risk. The trouble comes when someone gets careless, arrogant, or unlucky. Barry Seal was all three.

Adler Berriman "Barry" Seal was a pilot who smuggled drugs and weapons for the Medellín cartel. He also dabbled in dealing and money laundering. Some of his early instructors considered him a flying prodigy and becoming a professional pilot seemed a given. After serving in the National Guard and Army Reserve, he was hired by TWA, becoming one of the youngest to fly a Boeing 707.

A bit of a rogue, acquaintances later remembered him as wild, fearless, and mostly unconcerned with the consequences of his actions. A less charitable observation was that Seal wasn't as smart and clever as he thought he was. One acquaintance summed him up as *full of fun, full of folly*.

His first run-in with the law was in 1972 when he was one of eight people arrested for a plot to smuggle explosives out of the United States. He wasn't convicted, but TWA fired him anyway. By 1976 he was supporting himself by smuggling marijuana, and within a couple of years, he moved on to cocaine, which was more compact and not as vulnerable to drug dogs. And it was more profitable because the risks were so much greater.

Seal and the pilots he recruited trafficked drugs over the Louisiana border, pushing packed duffel bags of cocaine out of his plane into the Atchafalaya Basin, America's largest river swamp. The DEA became aware of Seal and after watching him for years, eventually secured an indictment against him in March 1983, charging him with conspiracy to distribute methaqualone and possession with intent to distribute Quaaludes. He was arrested in Florida, tried, and sentenced to ten years in federal prison. Soon after the sentencing, he went to the DEA to ask to become an informant. His first efforts to make a deal by giving the US information on the Ochoa family was rejected. But in March 1984 Seal was finally able to get a deal.

Some say Seal had started working with the CIA as far back as the late 1970s, gathering intelligence by flying low over Guatemala and Nicaragua during his smuggling runs and snapping photos from his plane. It's also rumored that the CIA turned a blind eye to Seal's drug smuggling in exchange for him delivering weapons to Nicaragua for the Contras, who the US government was helping to fight the Sandinistas government, which was technically socialist and not communist, but that was close enough for Reagan.

According to *Smuggler's End: The Life and Death of Barry Seal*, written by a retired FBI agent named Del Hahn, the only confirmed connection between Seal and the CIA occurred in 1984 after Seal had begun working as an informant for the DEA. The CIA placed a hidden camera in Seal's plane on a trip to pick up a cocaine shipment in Colombia. Seal and his copilot were able to obtain photographs that proved a link between the Sandinistas and the Medellin cartel, key intelligence for the Reagan administration's plans to help overthrow the Sandinistas' regime.

Although he dealt with lieutenants of the Medellín cartel, Hahn claims Seal didn't actually meet the Ochoa brothers or Pablo Escobar in person until the mid-1980s when Seal was working with the DEA on the sting operation. But the plans to capture the cartel leaders went down in flames after Seal's status as an informant was revealed in a *Washington Times* cover story. There are people who believe a certain Army colonel leaked the story to reveal the Sandanistas's involvement in the drug trade, making Barry collateral damage. Who knows?

Despite cooperating and doing informant work for the government, Seal's charges were not fully dismissed. He was sentenced to probation and had to spend six months at the Baton Rouge Salvation Army treatment center. On the evening of February 19, 1986, while getting out of his car at the center, Seal was reportedly killed by Colombian hitmen armed with machine guns. Officials suggested Jorge Ochoa, a founding member of the Medellín cartel, had ordered the hit. The three alleged shooters were arrested and given life sentences.

If there is a moral to Seal's story, it's don't get caught. And if you do, keep your mouth shut. But if you sing, just pray a newspaper—or former military associate—doesn't out you.

Our operations base in Freeport, Grand Bahama Island

Flashback, Norman's Cay[2]

In a part of the world where drug smuggling was as common as balmy breezes, Norman's Cay stood out as especially notorious for being the Medellín cartel's short-lived flight hub for drug smuggling. Located in the Bahamas's Exuma island group east of Nassau and two hundred miles from Florida, Norman's Cay is just a few hundred acres but was plenty big enough to run a major cocaine distribution business from.

The official story is that Medellín cartel co-founder Carlos Lehder bought a house on the island in 1977 and over the following years bought essentially every property on the island. Anyone who resisted selling were soon convinced it was in their life's best interest to take the money and run. Once he had control of the island, Lehder spent $5 million to lengthen the airstrip and improve the dock.

He started his cocaine operation in 1978, smuggling product to Florida and Georgia. He hired armed guards to patrol the island in Jeeps and helicopters. Visitors were made very not welcome, but for invited guests Norman's Cay was like a strip club theme park. One of Lehder's friends recalled his first visit in a *Frontline* documentary.

---

[2] Cay: a small, low lying island

I recall one of my first visits to the island... I remember, specifically, getting out of the airplane, the plane hasn't even stopped taxiing on the runway, and this Land Rover pulls up, and ...a very beautiful naked woman is driving, and she's going to welcome me. So when you open the door to the plane and you find this beautiful lady naked, you say, wow, this is the place to be.

Norman's Cay was a playground; it was a Sodom and Gomorrah, Drugs, sex, no police—you made the rules. We partied, and it was fun.

It didn't take the DEA long to sniff out, so to speak, the comings and goings on Norman's Cay. The Feds organized a task force that set up surveillance on nearby Shroud Cay. In September 1979, nearly three hundred Bahamian police officers raided Norman's Cay, arresting dozens of the cartel's worker bees. Lehder was apprehended trying to flee the island because a Bahamian official had warned him the raid was about to happen.

The heads up also meant there were no drugs to be found when the police arrived. Lehder is said to have paid $250,000 to an official to speed up the inquiry, and within two days he and his men were back on

Norman's Cay. One DEA official groused that Lehder not only owned Norman's Cay, but he owned "the whole damned country."

The unofficial version. Lehder was working in cahoots with the CIA, who had already started supporting the Contras, which is why the DEA always seemed a step behind.

Anyway, the DEA started arresting Lehder's pilots and seizing his shipments. The Feds eventually indicted Lehder and thirty-one others, and in July 1982 Lehder left Norman's Cay and became a fugitive on the run, going from Colombia to Cuba to Nicaragua and back to Colombia, where he was captured in 1987—and by many accounts was certifiable between suffering from cerebral malaria and waaaay too much cocaine. Lehder was extradited to the US, tried for trafficking, convicted, and sentenced to life without parole plus 135 years tacked on for good measure. But in 1992 he agreed to provide testimony against Panamanian dictator Manuel Noriega in exchange for a reduced prison sentence of fifty-five years.

After Lehder's arrest, his property on Norman's Cay—which was essentially the entire island—was confiscated by the Bahamian Government. Today it is a popular tourist destination reachable by charter flights that use the well-kept airstrip. The wreckage of a sunken C-46 cargo plane that an over-served pilot guest of Lehder's crashed in shallow water while trying to land after going for a drunken joy ride is a top attraction for snorkelers, a relic of days long gone by.

Chapter Seven: Recruited by a Government Agency

After a short but well-deserved vacation on an island where the natives were friendly, I returned to Freeport to supervise the work on a newly acquired old DC-3 at our maintenance and overhaul facility known as the Bahamian Skunk Works. The MX Aircraft crew there were experts in building world-class smuggling aircraft.

One day two gentlemen showed up at our facility. Their names were Mr. RK and his father Mr. HK. They asked for me by name.

Mr. RK said, "My father needs a copilot on our DC-6 tomorrow."

I laughed. "Sorry, I don't fly copilot. And the money is not important."

As they left our hanger, the father, a hardcore Texan, said to his son, "I like that kid, and I want a fly with him."

And one day, he would.

#

A meeting of all the players in our operation, and then some, had been scheduled for the following week in Nassau at the Britannia Beach Hotel on Paradise Island. It was a roundtable of sorts with aircrews, boat crews, ground personnel, management, and even some cartel accountants.

I arrived in Nassau the night before and secured the hotel's penthouse for the flight crew—winner, winner, chicken dinner. That evening before the meeting I had dinner with some of the Colombian cartel accountants at the Nassau Beach Casino.

As we were walking through the casino, one of the accountants said, "There's one of our guys at the craps table. We want to introduce you to him."

The man was wearing a loud—to the point of deafening—sport jacket and had obviously been seriously over-served. He was yelling and throwing black $100 chips all around the craps table.

We walked up, and the accountant introduced me to the man. It was Barry Seal.

I turned to the accountant. "Get me away from this guy; he's attracting way too much attention."

So we left. At the time Barry Seal was flying for the accountant's boss, El Jefe. He was also flying for the agency by then. He was the poster boy for the dangers of getting in over your head and turning informant, a bad move on his part.

After Barry's death, I once asked El Jefe's right-hand man, Carlos, what had really happened. He told me Seal's murder was made to look like the cartel was responsible, but says they were not. Draw your own conclusions.

#

The meeting was held the next day, and it felt more like a convention because all the factions were represented. Even the Feds were there.

Our flight crew met in the hotel café along with the boat people, the Blue Dolphin Gang. I was seated in a booth next to Al, the Super Ratón. Across from him was our Cuban radio operator. Across from our table was the leader of the Blue Dolphin Gang. His nickname was Mud Bone.

I noticed there were three men in sport jackets and Bermuda shorts at the opposite end of the café. One of them came over and sat down across from me.

"Hi, Doctor; my name is unimportant," he said, then told me he was with one of the alphabet soup agencies. "The other two gentlemen with me are also from the agency, and this conversation is being recorded."

I looked over at Mud Bone, who was doing the full felony turn— looking the opposite direction from us on purpose to hide his face.

I asked the agent, "What can I do for you?"

"We would like to send you to Bolivia to learn how to smuggle cocaine into the US."

Al piped up, in a heavy Spanish accent, "I don't think he needs to go to school for that."

Ha!

The agent didn't smile. "We don't think so either. We know you're returning to Freeport tonight. There will be an MU-2 turboprop corporate aircraft parked in front of your DC-3 at exactly 3:00 p.m. tomorrow. We suggest you get on it to go for an interview."

At that all three agents left the café. Mud Bone turned toward me, looking white as a ghost.

"That guy was my intel section commander in Laos, Cambodia, during the Vietnam War," he said. "You better make that meeting, or bad things could happen."

We returned to Freeport later that evening. The next day I started in on a case of Heineken round 2:00 p.m. By three o'clock I was on my last six-pack as I walked toward our DC-3. There was the MU-2 turboprop parked in front of it. Two men in black (MIB)were standing in front of the MU-2. They were literally dressed in black suits, white shirts, black ties, and sunglasses so dark, as ZZ Top would say, they didn't even know their names. As we climbed into the MU-2, the copilot said to get in and sit down.

Refreshments were not served.

We took off for an supposedly unknown (to me) destination. We flew an ever-changing course all over for maybe an hour and a half, the pilots obviously trying to disorient me, while I was watching the flight instruments from the back.

We were on final approach to some island when I stuck my head in the cockpit between the two MIB.

"Oh, yeah, that's Normand's Cay," which was less than forty-five minutes from Freeport. "What happened? Did you guys get lost?"

MIBs don't have much of a sense of humor.

We landed and pulled up to a large hangar whose doors were closed. The pilot shut down the engines.

The copilot turned toward me. "Get out and walk toward the hanger doors."

I was thinking: *Okay, this is where I get shot.* I had brought that six-pack with me, and I was on my last beer. As I walked toward the hangar, the doors opened. Inside three men were sitting behind a table. In front of the table was an empty chair. One of the men told me to sit down.

I had just read *Interrogation: Techniques and Tricks to Secure Evidence* from Paladin Press. This set up was a textbook interview/interrogation. The guy in the middle asks the questions or relays the information while one of the others is the bad cop, and the third is the good cop.

The man in the middle said, "Doctor, we want you to fly for us. You'll be flying two weeks on and two weeks off. We'll pay you $10,000 per night. We suggest you live outside the United States; most of our pilots like Hong Kong."

He explained the trips would originate from Norman's Cay, with the plane loaded with cocaine. I'd fly to Mena, Arkansas. The same city where a certain agency had allegedly set Barry Seal up with his very own airport. I did have the uncomfortable sensation I was following in his footsteps. Anyway, after unloading the cocaine in Mena, we would return to Norman's Cay.

From what I was told that day in Norman's Cay, the operation was started by the agency—and I suspect in concert with Colonel N—as a direct result of Congress cutting off funding to the Contras. The proceeds from this covert activity would be used to arm and resupply the Contras.

After their presentation I said thanks, but no thanks and turned down the job. Yes, the money was really good, but being alive is much better. If you got involved with cocaine, you were dealing with a whole different level of scary people.

I later heard that the guy sitting in the middle at the interview table on Norman's Cay was the brother of fugitive financier Robert Vesco. In 1973 Vesco absconded with a minimum of $224 million he looted from an offshore, Geneva-based mutual fund, equivalent to $1 billion in today's money. He ran after being indicted for making a secret $200,000 cash donation in April 1972 to President Nixon's infamous committee to re-elect the president (CREEP). That payment in part financed the Watergate burglary. At the time I was in Norman's Cay turning down the job offer, the US Marshall Service was still actively hunting Vesco, who had rented an island—the entire island—off the south coast of Cuba from Fidel Castro.

One thing about being a pirate; it was never dull.

#

After returning from another vacation, the Super Ratón and I were approached again by the agency. This time they requested that we fly in support of their covert wet teams. And this time we said yes. Although we were mercenaries, we were still patriots.

The Plan

The op started with relocating a DC-3 to Nassau. We were to arrive at exactly midnight. The tower operator at the Nassau airport had been paid to turn off all runway and airport lighting five minutes prior to our

135

arrival. We arrived on time with all of our lights out as well. It had recently rained, and the runway had a sheen on it from the reflected moonlight. We landed and taxied to a prearranged spot and parked.

As Al and I deplaned the DC-3, we were immediately surrounded by eight to ten Nassau Bahamian police. My first thought was: *Great; we're going to be sleeping on a concrete floor tonight.*

A young Bahamian man around my age walked up wearing a beige Pierre Cardin suit and sporting a solid gold Rolex. He introduced himself as the chief of police on the island.

"How is the food in jail?" I asked.

The chief laughed. "You're not going to jail; you're staying at the Cable Beach Hotel, and I'm here to escort you there."

"Uh, the hotel is still under construction and is not open yet."

"The penthouse is."

The First Trip

Our first mission was to airdrop a heavily-armed, five-man team behind hostile enemy lines in Nicaragua and then return alive. We nicknamed our operation Adios Airlines, an homage to one of my favorite movies, *High Risk,* which has some great DC-3 scenes.

Anyway, we boarded the DC-3 before 7:00 a.m. when the Feds came to work at the airport.

Al announced, "I want to be the captain today."

I laughed. "Okay, get in the left seat."

As we taxied out to the runway, the five-man mercenary team already had their full war gear on. Then Murphy's law struck again when the landing gear warning horn sounded.

I told Al, "Look out your window and check the left landing gear," as the wheel was visible from the cockpit.

I looked out my side window. "Uh, Al, I found the problem." I pointed out my side window with my lips, in true Puerto Rican style. "The right engine is on fire."

"What kind of fire?"

While white smoke is an indication of an oil fire. Black smoke is a fuel fire; that's the bad one that can kill you. This was an oil fire, with heavy white smoke pouring out 360 degrees from around the right engine cowling. An engine oil line had come off and was spraying oil all over the hot back engine cylinders, burning the oil.

This did not go unnoticed by the airport control tower operator. He immediately sounded the alarm with the airport fire station. We parked the DC-3 on the covert-side of the ramp with the other junk aircraft just as two airport firetrucks arrived. Before deplaning to talk with the firemen, I told the five-man team to stay in the airplane because I had this.

The DC-3's right engine was still spewing thick smoke as two Bahamian firemen were approaching the front of the plane, both dressed in full fire suits. When I came out they removed their fireproof hoods and started shouting orders.

"Get everyone out and away from the burning plane!"

I explained that there was no fire, just some oil burning off. A very brief argument ensued until the firemen looked over my shoulder, then turned to each other.

One said, "He's right; there's no fire. Let's get the hell out of here."

I had my back to the DC-3. When I turned around I saw all five team members standing behind me in full camo, their hands in large black tactical bags. That would be where they keep the MP-5 machineguns.

I looked at them and asked, "What part of: *Stay in the airplane* didn't you get?" The Super Ratón now walked up and joined the party. "You guys have ten minutes to escape. I'm in control of the airport police but not the military, and they will be here in force in ten minutes."

I bid them good luck then Al and I headed for our Plan B escape pod: we had parked a small, twin-engine aircraft close by a couple of days earlier for just this kind of emergency. We flew back to Freeport, Grand Bahama, then airlined home. I went to the West Coast, and Al went back to Puerto Rico.

The Second Trip for the Agency

The Super Ratón and I arrived in Nassau by commercial airlines from our respective homes. Shortly after checking into the hotel on Cable Beach, we had a visitor to our luxury two-room suite. It was the police chief.

"Doctor, you cost me a lot of money last time you were here."

"How is that?"

"Those five men escaped," he said.

"How is that possible?"

"I don't know. My police force was already at the airport, and the military forces arrived right after you and Al took off."

"So what can I do for you?" I asked.

"You're flying the same team tomorrow. Find out how they escaped so we can get money from them."

Right. "I'll inquire," I promised, "but no guarantees."

The next morning before 7:00 a.m. as we had prearranged through cash donations to the airport police, Al and I were outside pre-flighting the old Adios Airlines DC-3.

The five-man team appears out of nowhere. As they are stowing their gear in the bird, Al and I walked up to the team leader and his XO (second in command).

"How did you guys get off the island last time?" I asked.

The XO piped up. "We swam, sir."

Al starts laughing.

"Excuse me, sir. Did I say something funny?"

I told the XO Al was laughing because the nearest island was about seventy miles away.

The commander nodded. "Roger that."

#

This mission was to be a daylight parachute drop from altitude at quite a distance from the intended target. The flight went as planned. On the way to the initial point of the drop (IP), the commander and the XO were in the cockpit talking with us.

I said, "I think you gave me the wrong coordinates."

The commander pulled out an electronic device about the size of a modern laptop, does some calculations on it, then says, "Nope. You're on target."

I asked him if his device was a portable electronic boat navigation system. We had one installed in the aircraft, but I knew it didn't work in that part of the world.

Hi smiled. "Something like that."

I suspect it was GPS before anyone knew about GPS.

I told the team leader, "I've been down there before with the other side, and you're a good twenty miles from the nearest jungle village, and there are animals down there will want you for dinner."

I mentioned the large black panthers and the smaller jaguars that can climb any tree you'd be sleeping in. There were also fer-de-lance snakes in the jungle, a poisonous pit viper whose bite will kill unless you get anti-venom within twenty minutes.

The team leader smiled again. "Don't worry; we eat them."

Okay then, Mr. Bad Ass. "So, what if you were ratted out, and they kill all five of you guys?"

"We're the best-trained and best-equipped force on the planet with the best intel. Also, the bad guys don't know we're coming, and we're going to kill them from one thousand yards."

At that the XO interjected, "We don't always kill them from one thousand yards. We like to have fun too."

As we came over the drop zone, I got on the aircraft PA system and announced thirty seconds to jump time. "And thank you for flying Adios Airlines. And adios."

After the team jumped, the Super Ratón and I flew the bird back to another Bahamian island and abandoned the DC-3.

Postscript

We would later fly this same team to another mission, but I noticed one of the original members was missing.

I asked the commander what had happened to the guy.

He looked at me. "You were right about them jaguars ..."

Delivering El Jefe's Plane

On my return from the Caribbean, while transiting through Miami Customs, I was intercepted by an elderly female Customs agent, who read me the riot act and sent me to Station #8 for a strip search. I would cross paths with this same woman several more times in the future, and with each encounter her dislike of me would get progressively worse.

While I was in the United States, I was contacted by one of El Jefe's emissaries. He relayed to me that El Jefe had requested that I deliver his new personal aircraft: a twin-engine Piper Navajo with a Colemill Panther conversion, which meant installing bigger engines and four bladed propellers to optimize the power/weight ratio of the small-body Navajo..

I agreed to take the job and was to return to Miami for flight training in the Piper.

On my arrival at Miami International Airport, I was met by an old friend: Miami Mike's Ecuadorian company pilot. Mr. F would be my flight instructor for the Navajo training. After a couple of days flying the Navajo around the local Florida area, I was ready for the trip.

El Jefe had previously owned another Navajo that had crashed in the Colombian jungle. He was not on board at the time. Apparently he had loved that plane because his new Navajo was painted the exact color as the first. He didn't want a replacement; he wanted a clone. Upon delivery of the new Navajo to Colombia, his maintenance crew would repaint the registration number and change the data plates to match the old Navajo's, as though the old plane was never lost.

El Jefe really was an eccentric; Colombia's own Howard Hughes. That's what too much money, isolation, and paranoia gets you.

Anywho …

The Plan

The trip would start at Miami International, and I was to file a flight plan to Cape Haitian, Haiti, our then-base of operations, where I would spend the night. The following evening before departing for Colombia, I would pick up two passengers: a new copilot and a Colombian navigator who knew where the landing strip was in Colombia.

The trip to Cape Haitian went without a hitch. So far, so good. I filed a phony flight plan under another pilot's name from Cape Haitian to the Dominican Republic. The plan was to take off from Cape Haitian, fly south splitting the border of Haiti and the Dominican Republic directly to Cabo Rojo, and then as the crow flies to Colombia.

The plan worked, and we arrived at a remote but paved airstrip just outside Medellín, Colombia, around 2:00 a.m. At the end of the paved strip was what looked like a large hangar with the door open and lights on inside. A crane rumbled out of the hanger then we rolled in and shut down the engines as the hangar door closed behind us.

After about forty-five minutes of post-flight and unloading the aircraft of the special electronic equipment we had brought with us, the copilot and I exited the hanger to a waiting black, bulletproof SUV. Before getting into the vehicle, I turned to look at the hanger once more, and to my amazement it was camouflaged as a large house with fake doors and windows. I then saw faux electrical and telephone lines coming out of the "house" running to telephone poles down the side of the strip that hadn't been there when we landed earlier. Very *Twilight Zone*.

I walked over to one of the telephone posts. At the base was a round, concrete culvert with pipe buried about five feet deep that the telephone post was loosely set in. The Colombians had used that big crane to pull out the posts and lay them down just before we landed.

El Jefe's estate, Hacienda Napoles, was a little over ninety miles east of Medellín and 150 miles northwest of Bogotá. The three-hour SUV ride there was uneventful except for a couple of military checkpoints, and we arrived around 4:00 a.m. I was escorted to my room upstairs in the two-story mansion by an armed guard with an AK-47.

I was awakened at 9:00 a.m. by a butler in a white waiter's jacket, who was accompanied by my armed bodyguard. The butler handed me a small cup of Colombian coffee and a white bathrobe.

While I put the bathrobe on, the butler opened the plantation style balcony doors. I stepped out onto the veranda and to my surprise and enjoyment there were about eight nubile Colombian ladies swimming topless in the pool.

The butler asked, "Doctor, will you be having breakfast at the pool?"

"You think?"

The butler then opened the doors to a large walk-in closet filled with clothes—shirts, pants, sport jackets—all my size. Seeing my expression, the butler informed me with a smile, "Yes, Doctor, we know exactly what size you are."

As my bodyguard escorted me through the house to the pool, I noticed all kinds of different guns mounted on the walls.

The bodyguard smiled. "Take any gun you want and shoot anything you want, but you cannot shoot the animals."

I opted not to take any.

We also passed several large rooms, one with a full bar and two beautiful Latino ladies—also topless—playing snooker on a hand-crafted table. They smiled and told me to come play with them sometime.

I was eating my breakfast at the pool when the butler walked up with three heavily-armed guards.

"Mr. Carlos requests your presence."

Alrighty then. Walking through the estate grounds was like walking through Jurassic Park; it was filled with all kinds of exotic animals that were free to roam. It was hard not to worry about something jumping out at you.

Carlos, El Jefe's right-hand man, was dressed for business, wearing a sport jacket. Before we could exchange pleasantries, his two-meter radio crackled to life. He smiled and held it out.

"It's El Jefe for you."

The voice over the radio said, "Doctor, I understand all you care about is money."

I had made it clear we were mercenary pilots, so we didn't play favorites, and we were working for the agency also.

Carlos, still smiling, said, "Now, Doctor, be careful what you say as it might be the last thing you say."

On cue the three guards all jacked a 7.62 mm round in their AK-47s. Intimidate much?

I told El Jefe, "It's all about the money." I didn't get shot immediately, so that was a good sign.

El Jefe waxed philosophical. "Doctor, you know (which sounded like ju-no), when people tell me they want to be my friend, I seem to have a problem. But money is no problem. You know, we are not buying a service; we are buying a result. Have a nice time on my ranch."

Hospitality served with a warning to put me on notice. Like I said before, scary people. By that time, Barry Seal was already swimming with the fishes.

Carlos, who I called Lehi, said, "Doctor, we want you to fly for us and the Sandinistas, and we will pay you the same as flying our product."

I said okay. I never got to that snooker game. Shortly after that conversation the copilot and I were transported to the Medellín airport to airline back to Miami. The copilot, me, and one of El Jefe's handlers arrived at the Avianca Airlines ticket counter, where we presented our passports.

The counter agent frowned. "Where is your entry stamp into Colombia? How did you get here?"

I turned around to look at the arrivals and departures board behind me. I saw Avianca #809 from Miami to Medellín. I turned back to the agent. "We arrived on Avianca flight 809 yesterday."

The official stared at me. "Mister, that flight didn't fly yesterday."

Oops, I did it again.

Everyone behind the counter took off at a dead run toward the airport police station, but El Jefe's man managed to cut them off. He opened his briefcase and handed everyone large sums of cash. Everyone returned to the counter, and we received our tickets to Miami along with an apology.

"It must have been our fault for not stamping your passports inbound. Have a nice day."

The copilot and I arrived in Miami, and as we were clearing Customs there was my nemesis, the mean old Customs lady. We made eye contact.

So guess who got sent to Station #8 and strip searched?

Flashback, 1986

On Sunday, Oct. 5, 1986, a Fairchild C-123K cargo plane crashed in Nicaragua near the Costa Rican border. Later accounts would state a young Sandinista soldier brought the plane down with a surface-to-air missile. Whatever the cause, three of the C-123's crewmembers—William J. Cooper, Wallace "Buzz" Sawyer, and radio operator Freddy Vilches—were reportedly killed in the crash. The fourth passenger survived. His name was Eugene Hasenfus, and his subsequent capture by Sandinista forces led to the unraveling of a complex web of government deceit known as the Iran-Contra Affair.

Eugene Hasenfus was a former Marine who had flown supply missions for Air America, the CIA's air-transport company, during the heady days of the Vietnam War. Flash forward a few years. An old colleague at Air America encouraged him to come work for the covert airline. Hasenfus went to El Salvador to join the Contra resupply operation headed by Gen. Richard Secord for a promised salary of $3,000 per month, a lot more than he was making as a part-time construction worker in his hometown of Marinette, Wisconsin. His job was to kick the loads of cargo out the doors of the plane as it flew low over Contra-controlled areas inside Nicaragua.

On October 5, 1986, a C-123 Provider cargo plane left Ilopango Airbase in El Salvador loaded with seventy Soviet-made AK-47 rifles and 100,000 rounds of ammunition, rocket grenades, and other supplies.

As the plane entered Nicaraguan airspace it dropped to an altitude of 2,500 feet near San Carlos, along the Río San Juan. That's when the young Sandinista reportedly fired his shoulder-mounted missile, and the plane spiraled toward the ground. Unlike his colleagues, Eugene Hasenfus had a parachute that he had borrowed from a brother who was a skydiver. He jumped. The others on the plane went down with it.

The October 8 edition of the Sandinista newspaper *Barricada* featured a full-page cover photo of Hasenfus being led off by soldiers.

While it may have been "lucky" for Hasenfus to carry around a parachute, it ended up a problem for the CIA. In his 1991 autobiography *Hazardous Duty*, retired US Major-General John Singlaub, who was President Reagan's chief administrative liaison to the secret Contra supply effort, wrote: "Only a fool would dispatch such a plane on a clandestine airdrop during daylight. To make matters worse, Hasenfus and the three dead crewmen had been carrying their wallets with identity cards linking them to Southern Air Transport, a known CIA proprietary company. The final straw in this foul-up was the fact that the plane's logbooks were on board, which also linked the operation back to the CIA."

It was those logbooks, together with a business card found in Hasenfus' wallet when he was captured, that led to the public revelation of the US government's involvement in the Contra resupply operation.

The business card belonged to Robert W. Owen, who in 1983 joined Lt. Col. Oliver North in his Project Democracy to aid the Contras. According to Singlaub's book, North and Secord had botched the operation and then later tried to blame it on him.

"Ollie North's grandiose self-image as a master covert operator had come back to harm the Contra cause."

In some judicial irony, Hasenfus would later unsuccessfully attempt to sue Secord in US federal court for negligence and breach of contract.

The revelations on US meddling in the Contra-Sandinista conflict led to an outcry in both the media and Congress because it broke the Boland Amendment, which had made it illegal to offer assistance to the Contras for the purpose of overthrowing the Nicaraguan government. The Boland Amendment specifically prohibited "funds available to the CIA and the DoD [Department of Defense] from being used in Nicaragua for military purposes."

The Hasenfus incident became less and less a focal point as the whole selling arms to Iran part of helping the Contras was uncovered. Congress initiated an investigation to figure out what exactly the US intelligence agencies and Reagan's administration had been up to.

The Iran-Contra hearings began on May 5, 1987, and lasted through the summer until early August. Special Counsel Lawrence Walsh summarized the results: "Of the fourteen persons charged criminally during the investigation, four were convicted of felony charges after trial by jury, seven pleaded guilty either to felonies or misdemeanors, and one had his case dismissed because the Administration refused to declassify information deemed necessary to the defendant by the trial judge. Two cases that were awaiting trial were aborted by pardons granted by President Bush."

In 1988 Lt. Col North was convicted of obstructing Congress during its investigation, destroying government documents, and accepting an illegal gratuity. Those convictions were overturned in 1991 after an appeals court found that witnesses may have been swayed by testimony North had given in the televised hearings on the promise that it would not be used against him in court.

Outgoing President George H.W. Bush ultimately pardoned six of the key figures in 1992.

And Eugene Hasenfus? After being tried, convicted, and pardoned by the Nicaraguan government, he returned home to his wife and three children in Wisconsin. His father was quoted in the press at the time as saying, "It would have been better if Eugene had died. The dead don't talk."

The cost of his legal defense was never paid by the US government since officials were still trying to deny he was their employee. He struggled to find work, and the bank foreclosed on his house. He sued his employers, Southern Air Transport and Corporate Air Services, saying they had verbally promised to cover all of his legal fees, but he lost the suit in district court and again on appeal.

His wife divorced him in 1998, and then in July 2000 Hasenfus was accused of indecent exposure in Brookfield, Wisconsin. In June 2002 he killed a bear without a license and was fined $260. He was accused of lascivious behavior a second time in January 2003 after exposing himself in a grocery store parking lot. He was arrested a third time in 2005 for exposing himself in a Wal-Mart parking lot. This incident violated his probation and he served jail time in Green Bay, Wisconsin, until Dec. 17,

2005—the nineteenth anniversary of his release from the Sandinista prison.

Like Frank Wells before him, Hasenfus paid the price for crossing, even unwittingly, people in high intelligence places.

That's why to this day. I remember El Jefe's words: you're not paid for services, you're paid for results. In the mercenary world, your health and future depended on it.

Chapter Eight: The Guns of Grenada

By now it was time to take a long overdue mini vacation where the native girls were happy to see you and the beer was cold. But it would be a short-lived respite as my services were needed again by El Jefe. He had apparently made an agreement with some Colombian guerilla rebels— there are a bunch: the M-19s, Shining Path, Los Pepes, and FARC. What they have in common is wanting to overthrow the Colombian government.

The deal was, El Jefe would arm the guerilla fighters in exchange for them guarding his drug labs in the rebel-controlled Colombian jungle. The plan was orchestrated and executed by right-hand man Carlos, who was Ivy-League-educated and a former classmate of Fidel Castro's then-new head of intelligence. Carlos asked his old college friend if the Cubans or Russians would send armaments to Colombia for the rebels?

The answer was yes, but the Russians could not ship weapons directly to a sovereign country for a possible insurrection. They needed a transshipment point, so a large warehouse was built on Grenada to house the Soviet-manufactured weaponry that would be transported to Colombia. The warehouse was guarded by elite Cuban special forces trained by the Soviet special forces.

This is the story I later heard: The three Cuban soldiers from the warehouse facility went to town for a night of drinking and partying. They picked up three girls from the island's St. George's University. Apparently trying to impress the girls, the soldiers took them to the warehouse and showed off all the Soviet military hardware: tracked anti-aircraft guns, handheld surface to air rockets, cases upon cases of AK-47s, etc.

As fate would have it, one of the girls' father worked for the US Army at the Pentagon. She was well-informed about foreign armament. Sooo, she called Daddy to ask why all these Soviet-made weapons were on Grenada. Daddy had no idea, so he in turn called someone he thought would know: Marine Lt. Col N.

This went badly for the Cubans.

Before the Marines invaded Grenada, El Jefe had sent a Colombian ocean freighter/rust bucket to Grenada to pick up the armament. The hunk-of-junk ship broke down off the coast of Panama, and that's when I got the call. And my motto was: When you call, we haul.

The Plan

Our five-man crew would Learjet from Miami to Great Inagua where our super DC-3 would be waiting for us. We would then fly to Grenada, pick up a load of armaments, return to a covert strip in the Colombian jungle, and unload the cargo to the rebels.

Our crew was sitting in a Learjet at Butler Aviation on 36th St. at Miami International, and I had delayed the takeoff to wait for my catered seafood tray. As we were waiting, a Butler Aviation line boy stepped onto the Learjet.

"Is there a doctor on board?"

"Yes."

He looked skeptical but said, "There's a phone call for you."

Remember, this was in the days before cell phones; the first commercial cell phone wouldn't go on sale until the following year. So I went inside and picked up the phone.

The voice on the other end said, "Doctor, the mission is canceled. Go to the Marriot Hotel downtown—the penthouse has been reserved in your name—and turn on the TV news." Then he hung up.

We all went to the hotel, ordered room service—food and two cases of Heineken—then turned on the TV news. The Marines were invading Club Med, otherwise known as Grenada. If I had left Miami on time and not waited for my seafood tray, we might have landed the *New Millennium*

Falcon in the middle of a Marine invasion. And at that time I was playing for the wrong team.

A seafood tray very well saved my life.

By now I was considering retirement.

Fun (Probable) Fact

Another story told to me by the people in the know was that after the successful invasion of Grenada and the rescue of the college students, Colonel N had appropriated all the Russian armaments and transported it to Central America for the Contras.

#

I was in Los Angeles on Rodeo Drive shopping with a friend for covert electronics at CCS, (control communications systems), a full service surveillance and data systems integrator. The kind of place James Bond would shop at. I was looking to purchase a radio frequency bug detector.

As you walked into the store you encountered a vacant receptionist's desk—intentionally. On the wall behind the desk was a poster with a woman's face and the caption: *Are You Bugged?* What you couldn't see is the pinhole, fiber optic camera lens in her left eye that allowed the sales people to watch you from the back room.

Past the vacant reception desk is the showroom, where all the covert and spy equipment was laid out on tables. There were no sales staff on the showroom floor.

Then you'd make an ass out of yourself by telling your friend: "Gee, we could walk out with some of this stuff."

Wrong.

Just then the salesman came out and said, "Step into my office," where the video of you contemplating grand theft was playing on a screen.

Great sales gimmick, guys. I ended up buying a $16,000 RF bug detector that was built into a 2' x 2'x 6" silver Halliburton case. We wanted this equipment to sweep the aircraft for electronic bugs before and after takeoff.

Handy spook tip: When searching for bugs, remember they all have one thing in common: they need a power source.

#

After another short vacation where the local girls are friendly, it was time to head back to Miami. I was informed I would have a new boss and also a new copilot. I was to pick up the *New Millennium Falcon*, compliments of El Jefe, at Miami International near Corrosion Corner— sometimes referred to as Cockroach Corner—so-called because it was famous as an old airplane graveyard location and the site of many popular dive bars.

The *New Millennium Falcon* was a R4D—a US Navy designation—also known as a Super DC-3. The fuselage was lengthened by thirty-nine inches, it had a taller, rectangular tail, squared-off wing tips, and more powerful Pratt & Whitney R-2000s engines with 1,475 horsepower. A straight DC-3 engine has 1,200 hp.

I arrived in Miami and met up with my new copilot, Tim. He was from Coral Gables, Florida, and was about my age. I sensed we would work well together. Tim and I would ferry the R4D from Corrosion Corner at Miami Int. to Freeport, Grand Bahama for further covert aircraft modifications. Both before we left Miami and while en route to Freeport, I would run the RF bug detector.

And there were some, which was a strange feeling—but not unexpected.

On arrival in Freeport, a detailed inspection and debugging was the first order of business. The Feds liked to hardwire your emergency locater transmitter to the on position even when the switch is off.

After playing on the beach and drinking a lot of Beck's beer, the aircraft modifications were complete, and it was time to go back to work.

The Plan

The first trip for the Sandinistas was to fly the Super DC-3 from Haiti to a covert strip in Central America, pick up a load of weapons, then transport it to a clandestine location in Nicaragua.

The trip to Central America went as planned. On the second day after landing deep in the jungle of Nicaragua, we were informed that the fuel cart being pulled by farm animals was stuck somewhere due to mud slides on the trails and was two days from arrival. So there we were, stuck behind enemy lines in an active war zone.

And to think two weeks earlier I had been surfing in Newport Beach, California …

We were protected by an eight-man mercenary A-Team. Half were American and half were Central American. As I was walking from the DC-3 through the jungle to our temporary camp, I was carrying an M-16 machinegun and being escorted by five of the eight mercenaries. We started taking rebelfire from the treetop canopy, and I noticed it looked like they were shooting specifically at me.

When the shooting subsided I asked the team why the Contras were shooting at me. They all just smiled. One explained, "Because you're carrying an American M-16."

They all carried AK-47s.

"And when were you going to tell me that?"

"Better they're shooting at you than us."

Ha—not.

Mercenary tips: 1) When deep in country and behind enemy lines, carry the same gun as your enemy so when you "dispatch" them you can use their ammunition and not have to carry it. 2) Carry food and water. 3) Bring lots of Deep Woods Off.

The next day the farm-animal-transported fuel cart arrived. As the armaments were already loaded, we fueled and left, covered in lots of mosquito and other bug bites.

Over the next couple of months, we flew several armament supply trips for the Sandinistas. During one daylight trip we flew past a fresh aircraft crash site of a still-smoking C-123. I recognized it as a Contra aircraft. After we returned to our makeshift base camp in the Central American jungle, I called Carlos on the forty-meter Ham radio.

I asked, "Did the Sandinistas shoot down a Contra C-123?"

He said no.

I have no doubts it was the C-123K that Eugene Hasenfus had bailed out of. That crash ultimately ended up blowing the public lid off the Iran-

Contra operation. The Nicaraguan authorities had accused Hasenfus of working for the CIA, and he was sentenced to thirty years in prison for terrorism and other charges. Then a few months later Hasenfus, who claimed to be an airline cargo handler by trade, was pardoned and sent back to the United States.

Years later and while flying for the airlines, by chance I ran into a former pilot for Southern Air Transport who had known the captain of the C-123 that went down in Nicaragua. He said he was on the team that recovered the bodies.

"All three crewmembers had a bullet hole in the back of their head, and Hasenfus bailed out before the crash."

He surmised that one or all of the crewmembers were going to testify before a federal grand jury about the agency's gun and drug smuggling. He had no proof; this was just his take on the situation. It's moments like those that still give me pause.

Flashback, the Banality of Evil

Radical evil: a conscious choice to do something you know in

your heart is wrong.

Banal evil: engaging in is a behavior that has been normalized

by the society you live in.

The banality of evil is the theory—first suggested by author Hannah Arendt in her 1963 book about Adolf Eichmann, the Nazi considered the architect of the Holocaust—that the great evils in history generally, but particularly true for the Holocaust, were not carried out by fanatics or sociopaths, but by ordinary people who had been conditioned to normalize the unthinkable. Once something becomes a routine, daily occurrence, people eventually simply accept it as how things are done.

I guess you could apply that theory on a smaller scale to a wide swath of people including government agencies, cartels, henchmen, even mercenaries. It is certainly true for those who run third-world prisons.

Chapter Nine: Imprisoned in Haiti

After a couple of months in the Central American jungle we were released to return to the Rat's Nest on Cape Haitian. After landing in the *New Millennium Falcon*, I was approached by a military officer.

"The new colonel and the new chief of police wants to see you."

"What happened to the old colonel and chief of police?" I asked.

We'd been gone for several months; clearly, there'd been some changes.

He explained, "They shot the old chief of police, and the old colonel is in prison."

Before my brain could process the implications and set off alarms for me to turn around and fly off to wherever, the new Army colonel rolled up with his troops and announced: "You are all under arrest!"

Our entire five-man crew was loaded onto an Army truck with military armed guards and driven from Cap Haitian to Port-au-Prince, a harrowing six-hour drive over high cliffs on bad roads. At the time Baby Doc Duvalier—whose management style focused on murder and torture—was the country's dictator, which did not instill any confidence in what was going to happen. On the other hand, my rational brain felt assured that all would be well once our ransom was paid. Because make no mistake, this was your basic kidnapping.

Once in Port-au-Prince, we were taken to the Casan, the military wing of Baby Doc's residence. After hours of brutal interrogation, they decided to split us up. The radio operator, crew chief, and kicker would go to the hotel for house arrest. My copilot, Tim, and I would go to the Haitian National Penitentiary in downtown Port-au-Prince, where we would spend the next seven days, in between trips to the Casan for daily interrogations.

The Haitian National Prison could have been pulled straight from the movie *Midnight Express*, based on the true story of American college student Billy Hayes. On October 6, 1970, Hayes was caught attempting to smuggle some hash out of Turkey. The Turkish courts decided to make an example of him and sentenced Billy to more than thirty years in prison. Describing the facility as a hellhole is far too nice a picture. It was a squalid, brutal, inhumane dungeon. Over the week I was there I began to feel like I was actually in *Midnight Express: Haiti*.

That first night Tim and I arrived at the prison around 3:00 a.m., and I had managed to hide some US cash on me. I quickly and quietly bribed one of our guards to put us in the prison infirmary because it was the only place that had actual beds, nasty as they might be.

Right after laying down I heard scurrying from under my bed. I rolled over to look and saw the entire floor was awash with large rats. Didn't matter. I passed out from exhaustion, having been awake more than twenty-four hours.

Day one in the Haitian National Prison. I was awoken early in the morning by one of the prison guards violently shaking me. I opened my eyes and saw four armed guards pointing guns at me and speaking in French Creole. There was also an American with long gray hair wearing a Bandana and purple sunglasses leaning over me.

He said, "Doc, don't tell 'em anything."

His name was Robert Hall, and he'd been in prison for five years. He got busted in a Beechcraft-18 with a load of grass.

I was wearing shorts and a Harley Davidson T-shirt. When I sat up, I saw both of my legs had been chewed up by bed bugs. I paid the prison doctor to leave Tim and me in the infirmary. That doctor was as much of a real doctor as I was. It was a joke; they had a prison guard put on a white lab coat and pretend.

The prisoners that had money paid this fake doctor to stay in the infirmary. The other choice was a 40'x70' foot cell with seventy other prisoners, no toilet, and no way out.

Later that morning Tim and I were transported by a military escort from the prison to the Casan for more military style interrogation by the head of the Army, Colonel Paul, an older Haitian man with white hair. At one point they brought in a handcuffed Haitian man. Several military police officers beat him with clubs in front of Tim and me to get our attention. In a dictatorship there were no rules of fair treatment.

Day two was more of the same. The military guards would get Tim and me out of prison very early in the morning and transport us to the Casan. There they would make us sit on a hard, wooden bench next to a wall in an open-air atrium for about four to six hours before the interrogation started.

The atrium had four walls and was open to the sky. In the center was a ten feet tall, four-inch square post with a rope hanging down from the top, like a tetherball pole. Along another wall were what looked like 4'x3'x3' dog houses.

Day three was more of the same military interrogation. The focus of their questions was on where we had been before arriving in Cape Haitian.

I had an International Customs declaration, with a real Aruban departure stamp, that stated we had come from Aruba although we'd really come from Central America. The military tribunal wasn't buying our Aruba story, so it was back to prison.

Prison Life

In the Haitian National Prison, you were fed one meal a day: boiled cornmeal and eggplant. It looked like diarrhea; don't even ask what it tasted like. Limited food purposely kept the prisoners low on energy—an old trick. The toilet and shower in the infirmary had been out of service for at least the five years that Robert had been there. So you bathed by having someone pour a bucket of undrinkable water over you. As far as a bathroom, out in the prison yard against one of the walls was a three-hole outhouse.

At night around 7:00 p.m. we would be locked down in the infirmary, which has about twenty beds and an open, barred window spanning one entire wall.

The Entertainment

During the day the infirmary prisoners would gather fist-size rocks from the prison yard and stack them on the inside window ledge of the infirmary. Shortly after we were locked down at night, the rats would come out from everywhere and cover the prison yard. All of us prisoners would throw rocks at the vermin. We called it Robert's Rat Show.

Tim and I got a one-day reprieve from interrogation after a visit from a US embassy official. I was telling Robert Hall about the health club I went to in Newport Beach, California. He laughed and handed me two pieces of four-inch-square cardboard.

"Here are your workout gloves. Now come on outside to my club."

I followed him outside to the prison yard. We were doing some calisthenics then some jumping jacks in front of the outhouse. There was a prison guard with a rifle walking a catwalk around the inner prison yard wall. Every time the guard got to a certain point on the catwalk, Robert would yell out attention in French.

"Why are you yelling when the guard gets to that point on the catwalk?" I asked.

"What? Are you blind? We're tunneling out."

Right out of the old Steve McQueen film, *The Great Escape*, there was an escape tunnel in progress, and I would get to be part of it. How much fun was that! (Yes, prison changes you.)

Then he said, "Now that you know there's a tunnel, see if you can find the entrance."

After two days of inconspicuously searching so as not to arouse the prison guards' suspicions, I gave up.

Robert laughed in delight. "The entrance is in the shitter!"

It was genius because no guard would want to go in there. He showed it to me, and the engineering was amazing. It was an optical illusion. Walking into the outhouse and looking down into any of the three holes on the bench and you would only see the layer of dung about eight feet down.

Robert and his crew had removed the three-hole bench seat and installed hidden hinges. It looked like it was nailed down, but you could flip the bench seat up, revealing the tunnel entrance, which was dug into the prison wall at a downward angle. Totally cool and totally undetectable.

As previously mentioned, the day before we had been visited in prison by the US Consul in Haiti, an older gentleman accompanied by a smoking-hot woman in her mid-twenties.

As the Haitian military police came to collect Tim and me from our prison cell Robert said, "Doc, don't sign or tell them anything. This country is a dictatorship, and the US has no authority here, so they can't or won't do anything for you."

"Roger that."

The military police lead us into a plush room with carpet and upholstered chairs. In addition to the consuls was the police chief. Tim was almost passed out in a chair asleep, so I was answering the consuls' questions. They were trying to get Tim and me to sign a Freedom of Information authorization form, so they could look up our ass with a microscope.

I shook my head. "Our attorney has advised us not to sign anything."

The older counselor asked, "Who is your attorney?"

"Robert Hall."

The chief of police smiled.

Then the smoking-hot woman asked, "How are they treating you here?"

Tim jumps up out of the chair and says with sarcastic excitement, "How are they treating us here? I've lost weight, quit smoking, and don't have to answer the phone. I love it here."

At that the police chief laughed out loud. The two consuls looked miffed. The colonel thought that was cool and gave us the day off.

Day six and Colonel Paul was not happy with the interrogation progress. (My interpretation: the ransom money wasn't getting there fast enough to his liking.) It was time to give Tim and me an attitude adjustment. Five prison guards with guns drawn came into the infirmary and marched us to the nasty, rat-infested, pitch-black solitary cell. We called it the box. When the guards opened the cell door to push us in, a pack of really large rates ran to the back corner of the cell.

Can you say, eeeek?

The cell was an empty concrete cave with about a quarter inch of green slime and rat droppings covering the floor. There was nowhere to sit but on the floor. Once the guards slammed the cell door closed, it was totally dark. Just when you thought it couldn't get any worse, I soon felt rats running over my shoes.

Eeeeek and *eeeeek*.

After what seemed to be an eternity—but was only about two hours—the cell door opened. Again, the rats ran to the back of the cell, and we were escorted back to the infirmary.

Day seven. It was becoming like *Groundhog's Day*. Tim and I were again escorted from the penitentiary to the Casan. We were sitting on the now-familiar wooden bench in the atrium of the Casan. After a couple of hours had passed, eight Haitian soldiers arrived with a prisoner, who had a three-foot bamboo stick across his back and through his arms with his hands tied in front of him.

Two soldiers tied short ropes around the bottoms of his pant legs while another tied the long rope from the ten-foot pole to the middle of the bamboo stick behind his back. Then the three soldiers hoisted him up about a foot off the ground. All eight soldiers went over to a cabinet on the opposite wall, and each pulled out what looked like wooden ax handles with a square tops. They circled the prisoner and proceeded to play tetherball with him, using the wooden ax handles to propel him around the pole.

It was brutal, but Tim and I could only sit and watch. After the soldiers took away what was left of the prisoner, the police chief arrived. It was unusual to see a police officer there as this was a purely military facility. He escorted us to an office in the building. En route we walked past one of the small, concrete dog houses, and I noticed a pair of black hands holding onto the barred doghouse door from the inside.

I bent down and looked in. It was the Haitian man we had filed the phony flight plan with when we left Cape Haitian months ago. He was in bad shape, and it appeared he had also done his fair share as a tetherball on the pole.

The chief let us into a small office furnished with several chairs then left. He returned about fifteen minutes later with the man from the doghouse in handcuffs.

They sat down then the chief asked Tim and me, "Do you have anything to say?"

We both said no, believing we were next up on the pole. Instead the police chief smiled widely at us and announced, "Well, then, you two and the other three crew members will be going home tomorrow."

I asked the chief what had changed.

He pointed to the man from the doghouse. "He has confessed to filing false flight plans. So you see, we have our man."

In other words, our boss's money had finally arrived and been doled out.

Tim and I were escorted back to the penitentiary for the night. The next morning before departing I said my goodbyes to Robert but vowed to return soon to visit. Which I did.

I asked Robert what I could send him.

"I like novels."

"What kind of novels?"

Robert looked me square in the eye. "Escape novels."

God love the human spirit.

Tim and I were reunited with the other crewmembers on the tarmac of the Port-au-Prince International Airport. Still in handcuffs, we were all escorted by twenty armed Haitian soldiers onboard an Air Haiti B-737 airliner to Miami.

Tim and I boarded last. We were standing in front of all the first-class passengers while two soldiers took our handcuffs off and said, "Have a nice trip."

The expressions on the passengers' faces were priceless as Tim and I walked to the back of the cabin, especially since neither of us had taken a real shower in seven days!

In the cockpit of the DC-3, the Millennium Falcoln

Flashback, Baby Doc Duvalier

Over human history strongarm dictators have been a constant, dime a dozen reality, with literally too many to count. But some have stood out either because they were emblematic of the times they lived in, had a lasting historical impact, or were just especially batshit crazy. Such memorable despots include Vlad, the Impaler (sadistic cruelty), Hitler (genocide), and Caligula. (sexual perversions extreme even by Roman standards.)

In the 1970s and '80s, the dictator du jour was Haiti's Jean-Claud "Baby Doc" Duvalier, who was the focus of fascination largely for his narcissistic flamboyance, let-them-eat-cake leadership style, and an apparent obliviousness that having people killed just because they might disagree with you isn't acceptable or else we'd have no humans left on the planet.

He had become "president for life" in 1971 after the death of his father, "Papa Doc" Duvalier, who had never met a human right he didn't trample. Haitians initially welcomed Baby Doc, thinking anyone had to be less tyrannical than his father. But as the younger Duvalier matured, he consolidated the ranks of his civilian militia force, the Tonton Macoutes, who were fiercely loyal to the Duvaliers and merciless toward any opponent real and, more often, imagined. They were the Caribbean version of Nazi Germany's Gestapo. They had been formed to protect first Papa Doc and now Baby Doc from the Haitian Army, which had a long history of plotting coups and toppling dictators.

The Macoutes went about their business with absolute impunity, carrying out torture, extortion, and murder at will. Human rights groups estimate about fifty thousand Haitians were killed or disappeared during the Duvalier era.

Baby Doc fled Haiti in 1986 after political oppression/repression plus a collapsing economy combusted to set off violent rioting. He asked France for asylum and the United States for the plane to take him there, an American official said at the time. Haiti, already the poorest country in the Western Hemisphere, became even poorer because it is believed that by the time he left, Baby Doc had embezzled about $900 million from the country's treasury and sent it to Swiss bank accounts to subsidize his exile lifestyle. And the Tonton Macoutes? Its members were allegedly absorbed into the Army.

Baby Doc's departure set the stage for democratic elections four years later, won by a former priest, Jean-Bertrand Aristide, who eventually disbanded the aforementioned upstart army. But Aristide would be run out of Haiti himself in 2004 after a bloody coup d'etat supposedly orchestrated by the US and carried out by a group of former Haitian army members.

While Baby Doc was never accused of directly profiting from Haiti's drug smuggling activity, not long after his exile, Duvalier's father-in-law was indicted for working with a group that smuggled cocaine from Colombia through Haiti to the United States. But the members of that ring were later granted amnesty by the provisional government's minister of justice, who then resigned—one might imagine a much richer man.

Baby Doc died of a heart attack in 2014.

MIAMI HERALD
August 3, 2015

When Haiti flourished as a "narco-state," Colombian cocaine smugglers would pay off local cops to protect their precious loads flown in on planes that landed at night on dirt roads illuminated with the headlights of police cruisers, according to U.S. authorities.

On Monday, a federal prosecutor accused a veteran Haitian National Police officer of providing security for thousands of kilos of Colombian cocaine transported to the island that would eventually be smuggled into the United States.

Claude Thelemaque, a onetime police commander who was whisked away to Miami last November after his arrest at the U.S. Embassy in Port-au-Prince, is standing trial on a drug-trafficking conspiracy charge—the latest Haitian law enforcement officer to be taken down in a saga dating back more than a decade.

And the beat goes on.

Outside the wall of Haiti's National Penitentiary in Port-au-Prince

Chapter Ten: The Haitian Affair

After the usual Customs strip search in Miami, I flew to Portland, Oregon, rented a car, and drove fifty-four miles south to hang out with my on-again, off-again girlfriend Elaine in Salem. Elaine was a very nice girl with a mundane eight-to-five job and little idea of my true profession. Like in the Arnold Schwarzenegger movie *True Lies*, I told her I had a company that delivered aircraft all over the world, which was why I was often gone several months at a time.

Elaine lived in a modest, two-bedroom condominium that I financed for her, along with an unlisted landline phone number. This was in the days before cell phones. On the second day of my stay, the phone rang. I was standing there when Elaine answered it.

She looked at me, clearly miffed, and held out the phone. "They're asking for the Doctor but not really speaking English."

I took the phone. "Hello?"

"Doctor?"

Ah. I immediately recognized the mixture of English and French Creole. It was some Tonton Macoute minion of Baby Doc Duvalier. What I wanted to know was why a member of Baby Doc's murder squad was calling me. In Oregon. At my girlfriend's condo on her unlisted number.

But I said, "What can I do for you?"

"Colonel Paul wants to see you *tomorrow*."

I laughed. "The same colonel that was interrogating me at the Casan?"

"Yes. We have your first-class travel set up for tomorrow from Portland to Miami then direct to Port-au-Prince. The penthouse at the casino here is reserved in your name."

"What's the urgency?"

"The Haitian Air Force is for sale, and you're the only one the colonel can trust because you never talked."

I hung up and turned to Elaine. "Honey, I've got to go …"

Yeah, back to hell.

#

Before leaving Portland I stopped at some antique novelty stores there looking for a special gift that I wanted to take with me. I had this toy when I was a kid. It came in a round, brown jar with a screw off lid that was a little bigger than a large peanut butter jar. When you opened it, three green, springy snakes flew out like a jack in the box. I finally found one and then headed to catch my flight.

I was met at the Port-au-Prince International Airport by four Tonton Macoute wearing silk shirts and dress slacks in the afternoon. They looked like they had just come from a 1970s disco. I got in the back seat of an old, beat up, brown four-door Honda. I was sitting in the middle with a Haitian on either side and knee deep in AK-47s and ammo on the floor.

They drove directly to the Haitian Air Force base and blew by the front gate checkpoint not even slowing down. We pulled up in front of three uniformed officers on the Air Force ramp. Climbing out of the car I recognized Colonel Paul, the head of the Haitian Army. There was also another colonel who was the commanding officer of the Haitian Air Force and the commanding officer—also a colonel—of the Haitian Navy.

As I approached the officers, Colonel Paul smiled. "Doctor, it's nice to see you again under these different circumstances."

Ha. Ya think? I asked, "What can I do for you gentleman?"

The Air Force colonel said, "All the Air Force airplanes are for sale."

There were six brand new SIAI-Marchetti S211As—a two-seat jet fighter trainer—supplied to the Haitian Air Force by Italian aircraft manufacturer Aermacchi. Each had less than ten flight hours on them. I got in the front pilot seat of one and started it up.

The Air Force colonel said, "Take it up and fly it."

I laughed. Good way to meet your maker in a Marten Baker ejection seat. "Maybe I should read the flight manual first."

I noticed there were brand new flight suits and helmets in the hangar. I asked the Air Force colonel, "Where are all your pilots?"

He smiled. "The Haitian Air Force only pays the equivalent of $10 US dollars a month, so they all left for better jobs."

I then asked the three Colonels how much money they needed for the six SIAI-Marchettis. They said $300,000.

"That's all for each?" At that time these jets were worth $6 million each.

"No, we only need $100,000 US for each of us, and you can have all six aircraft. But you must fly them out of this airbase in disguise."

I, of course, said okay.

\#

Before I left Haiti I had a promise to keep: a long overdue visit with my friend Robert Hall. I made the trip back to the National Penitentiary where he was still incarcerated. But first I stopped at a local grocery store and loaded up with two large bags of food and other tradable items.

I arrived at the prison and bribed two of the guards to let me see Robert. They put me in an office then went to get him.

After he walked in I asked, "How's the tunnel?"

"Well, it was going great until we found out the prison used to be an old Spanish fort and the walls are fifteen feet thick."

I gave Robert the groceries, and we exchanged pleasantries. Then it was lockdown time, and I left. I was on my way to Los Angeles to meet a government agent about financing the Haitian jet transaction, but as usual had to stop in Miami to clear Customs.

Before leaving Port-au-Prince I had put my can of snakes in a shoe box, taped it with an entire roll of duct tape, then put it in my checked luggage. After deplaning in Miami I cleared immigration and retrieved my luggage in baggage claim. On the way to Customs, I stopped in the men's room and threw water all over my T-shirt, so it looked like I was sweating profusely. I made my way to Customs, and before walking up to my favorite Customs lady, I put on a pair of mirrored sunglasses.

I tossed my bag right in front of her.

She barely glanced at me. "You're good to go," she said, apparently not recognizing me.

I took off my sunglasses and looked right at her. "You don't want to check my bag?"

Now realizing it was me, she tore into my bag and soon pulled out the duct-taped brick. She held it up. "What's this?"

I shrugged. "I've never seen that before."

She ripped off the tape with her fingernails and teeth before another Customs agent gave her his knife. She eventually got down to the can then looked at me as she started to unscrew the lid. "I finally got you."

By this time quite a large crowd had gathered. When she pulled the lid off, and the snakes shot out, I said, "No, I got *you*."

I picked up my bag and walked out of Customs. Then spent that night in Miami celebrating before heading to LA the next day.

#

While in baggage claim at LAX, a government agent approached me. He said there was a limo waiting to take me to meet their covert finance and weapons supply guy. Once I plucked my luggage off the carousel, the agent escorted me outside to the curb and deposited me in the back seat of a black Lincoln Town Car. It was just me in the backseat and the driver up front.

We cruised into the heart of LA's manufacturing district. It wasn't long before the limo stopped at a rundown warehouse surrounded by an eight-foot cyclone fence with concertina barbed wire, the kind that comes in large coils that can be expanded like a concertina, a musical instrument in the same family as the accordion. There were also CCTV cameras around the top of the fence.

The driver opened my door, walked me up to the gate door, and said, "Push the intercom button. They're expecting you."

I followed his instructions, and a voice from the intercom said, "Walk into the warehouse."

It was late afternoon, and there were no lights on in the warehouse. The only illumination was from some opaque skylights. As I walked I could see piles of what looked like World War II bombs, old jet fighter engines, and large 4'x4'x4' wooden crates heaping with old handguns. Near the crates was a dark-complected man wearing a sport jacket. He nodded toward the crates of weapons.

"You didn't think the police and local government agencies really dump or melt down all those confiscated guns, now do you, Doctor?"

Apparently not. Without introducing himself he went on.

"You know, Doctor, we have been trying to get close to Colonel Paul for ten years. You spend seven days in the Haitian National Prison, and now you're his best friend. What's up with that?"

My answer was to produce Colonel Paul's business card with his personal phone number written on the back and hold it out. The man with no name took it.

"Doctor, we're going to finance you."

At that we said our goodbyes, and I left the facility. I contacted Colonel Paul the next day and told him the deal was on.

Colonel Paul, in concert with the Air Force colonel, shipped me the aircraft flight manuals for the S211As. For you pilot types, here are some aircraft specs.

Max speed: 414 knots at 25,000 feet.

Rate of climb: 5,100 feet per minute.

Five hardpoints for mounting under-wing armament

Two Marten Baker ejection seats.

Single engine JT15D-5 Pratt & Whitney, 3,190 lbs. of thrust.

The Plan

I rounded up some of my old pilot buddies from when I used to tow sky banners up and down the beach for Bob Cannon's aerial advertising company. At the time they were flying out of Meadow Lark Field in Huntington Beach, California.

After all six of us studied the S211A's pilot operating flight manuals, we would airline to Port-au-Prince International Airport. From there we would be transported to the Air Force base by the Tonton Macoute. Once at the aircraft hangar, we'd go to the fighter pilot ready room where we would don the new flight suits and helmets. Then with the dark helmet visors down and wearing the flame-resistant Nomex gloves, we would each board our fighter trainer that would be pre-fueled and pre-positioned on the Air Force ramp for us. We would fly to Great Inagua; the trainers had no external fuel tanks, and that was a safe range with some fuel reserve. After landing in Great Inagua, the S211A's wings would be de-mated, and the aircraft and wings would be loaded onto a prepositioned barge and shipped to the buyer, the Argentinean Coast Guard. It was something right out of the movie *Firefox*.

My end of the deal was $1 million split evenly between us six pilots minus expenses. Seeing how the six aircraft had a total value of somewhere in the neighborhood of $36 million, I would be doing more than my fair share of supporting a certain government agency's black ops program.

The colonel's money was ready, and it was only a few days until my five pilots and I would launch for Port-au-Prince.

Then I got the bad news. Jean-Claude "Baby Doc" Duvalier, Haiti's strongarm dictator, had fled the country in the face of increasing civil unrest against his rule. Apparently he believed a coup was only a matter of time, a day of reckoning long coming. No doubt the colonels had also seen the writing on the Tonton Macoute wall, which explained why they were looking to quickly get out of Dodge with some pocket cash. But the deal was no longer doable.

Bummer.

I later learned that Colonel Paul's maid poisoned him, causing him to come down with a bad case of dead. The Air Force colonel was summarily executed by firing squad. But the Navy colonel had managed to escape by sea for parts unknown.

One positive footnote: during the insurrection that followed, the rioting Haitian mobs blew up the National Penitentiary, enabling my friend Robert Hall to finally escape.

Ha!

The DC-6

Flashback, 1989

Even in a region rife with eccentric despots, Manual Noriega stands out. He claimed to speak for the people yet enjoyed a lavish lifestyle—mansions, bottomless cocaine, and a museum-worthy collection of weapons—all paid for by drug-trade earnings. He also liked to display his beloved teddy bears dressed as paratroopers. Despite his long association with the United States intelligence community, he was never truly trusted because the only thing he was loyal to was his own self-interest.

Noriega was born in a Panama City slum. Much about his early life is murky, like whatever happened to his parents. He told interviewers a godmother had raised him. Noriega attended the prestigious Instituto Nacional High School, and in a yearbook said his life's ambitions were to be a psychiatrist and president of Panama.

His plans for medical school apparently did not pan out, but he somehow got a scholarship to a military academy in Peru. When he returned to Panama, he rose through the ranks of the National Guard. In the late 1960s he became a protégé of dictator General Omar Torrijos Herrera, who signed a treaty with the United States in 1977 that stipulated America would cede control of the canal and the US property alongside it in December 1999. In his role as General Torrijos's loyal aide, Noriega arranged for the abuse and imprisonment of political opponents and other dissidents and helped tighten relationships with US law enforcement and intelligence officials.

After General Torrijos died in a plane crash in western Panama in 1981—there were some suspicious types who suspected it wasn't an accident and that Noriega might have been behind his mentor's death—Noriega took over the National Guard and became a general in 1983. Even though there was a civilian president, Noriega was the de facto strongman, uniting the various guard units under the Panama Defense Forces.

Noriega nicknamed himself *El Man*, but his detractors called him Pineapple Face—because of his pockmarked skin—and it was that nickname that endured, much to the general's irritation.

Fun fact: In October 2014, a California judge dismissed a lawsuit filed by Noriega protesting the use of his likeness and the Pineapple Face name in a *Call of Duty* video game. You don't become a dictator without having a healthy/psychotic ego.

Noriega used his power to rig elections, ensuring his handpicked candidates would win. He also strengthened ties to drug traffickers while simultaneously seeking to ally with the United States. He acted as an informant for a US agency or two then sold secrets gleaned from that to political enemies of the United States. For example, while providing secrets about Cuba to the United States, Noriega sold Fidel Castro thousands of Panamanian passports at $5,000 each, for use by Cuban and perhaps agents of other Soviet bloc countries. Even though many in Reagan's administration considered Noriega useful in helping keep tabs on various leftist uprisings in Central America, eventually his double-dipping prompted concerns in the US that hey, maybe this isn't the best guy to have on speed dial after all. The United States Senate in 1986 overwhelmingly approved a resolution calling on Panama to remove Noriega from the Panamanian Defense Forces pending an investigation of charges of corruption, election fraud, murder, and drug trafficking.

Hoping to stop his political freefall, Noriega reached out to Lt. Col. Oliver North and met with him in London during September 1986, just a month before Eugene Hasenfus's plane would crash and lead to the Iran-Contra revelations. We know this because the colonel kept journals that have since become public.

As we know, Colonel North was a key player in the Reagan administration's efforts to sabotage the leftist Sandinista government in Nicaragua by secretly selling arms to Iran and using the proceeds to finance rightist Nicaraguan rebels, known as the Contras. The subterfuge was necessary because Congress had banned funding the Contras.

The ever-helpful Noriega offered to assassinate Sandinista leaders or sabotage them in exchange for Colonel North helping Noriega repairing his standing in Washington. A later congressional report stated a sabotage plan had been approved, but there is no evidence Noriega ever carried it out. In 1987 Congress cut off military and economic aid to Panama.

Things weren't going much better at home for Noriega. After the 1985 torture and murder of Hugo Spadafora, a longtime critic who had publicly accused the general of working with Columbian drug cartels, opposition to Noriega grew among the John Q Panamanian public. In 1988 there was a demonstration against Noriega in Panama City followed by a failed coup. That prompted Noriega to become even more violent toward political opponents.

In a book about Noriega's rise and fall, the author noted that Noriega "craved power and became a tyrant; he craved wealth and became a criminal. And the careers came in conflict."

In 1988 Noriega was indicted in Miami and Tampa, Florida, on federal narcotics-trafficking and money-laundering charges. Specifically, he was accused of using Panama as a hub for shipping South American cocaine destined for the United States and allowing drug proceeds to be hidden in Panamanian banks.

His response was to go on the offensive. He organized anti-US demonstrations in Panama then in 1989 annulled the results of Panama's presidential election, daring the United States to stop him. After a second failed coup in 1989, he anointed himself *maximum leader,* and the National Assembly declared war on the United States.

In December 1989 President George Bush—the first one—approved an invasion force of more than 27,000 troops. Panamanian forces were quickly overwhelmed, and Noriega took refuge at the Vatican Embassy in Panama City. During the standoff, American forces blasted music outside the embassy to both torment Noriega and to prevent reporters with directional microphones from hearing conversations between the military and Vatican officials.

Noriega surrendered on Jan. 3, 1990, and was flown to a jail in Florida, while a new Panamanian president was sworn in on an American military base. Noriega's mug shot went viral. He was convicted in April 1992 and sentenced to forty years in prison, which was later reduced by ten years.

While imprisoned in the United States, the Panamanian government tried and convicted Noriega in absentia for the execution of soldiers in the failed 1989 coup attempt. And in July 1999, France tried him in absentia on money-laundering charges related to his drug profits. His lawyers argued that the money was actually a payment by the CIA, not drug earnings, but Noriega and his wife were convicted and sentenced to ten years in prison.

Between the various convictions, Noriega remained imprisoned in one country or another until his death on May29, 2017.

The authors of the book *In the Time of the Tyrants* sum up Noriega this way: "He craved power and became a tyrant; he craved wealth and became a criminal. And the careers came in conflict."

Noriega either didn't see or ignored what had become increasingly obvious as the 1980s wore on: the world was becoming an ever more complicated geopolitical place. What had started as dropping off some weed in exchange for a nice payday so people could get a cannabis high, had become part of a global chess game where governments had usurped the drug trade to fund their own political, military, and social agendas. The fall of the Berlin Wall and dissolution of the Soviet Union brought even more players into the equation, more agendas to fund. Noriega's biggest mistake was not knowing when to take his nest egg and go live out of sight on an island somewhere.

In the words of a famous country philosopher, you gotta know when to hold 'em, know when to fold 'em. And I knew my decade-long mercenary poker game was drawing to a close. Time to cash my chips in and move on.

Chapter Eleven: The DC-6 Trip to Panama

By the late 1980s my charter company based at the UCO jet center at the John Wayne Airport in Orange County, California, was doing well. It had been a wild theme park ride of a decade, but I had used up most of not all of my nine lives, and the world was changing. Communication technology was evolving exponentially, meaning it was going to be increasingly difficult to stay under the literal radar. The stakes were getting higher, and what had once been a grand adventure now seemed more like aerial Russian roulette. So I was considering retiring and returning to airline piloting.

Yes, it would be a pay cut, but better to be around to spend what you do have than to be in jail —or the ground.

I was sitting at my desk at our executive charter company—remember, I was the vice president (the doctor) of flight operations—when out of the blue Mr. RK who I had met while in Freeport, Grand Bahama Island, walked into my office.

He smiled and said, "You know, my father still wants to fly with you. And I have a proposition. Our DC-6 is parked at the Chino Airport," which was about an hour drive from Orange County. "We have sold it to some Mexican nationals who'll take possession of the aircraft in Panama.

But the DC-6 is in need of some heavy maintenance, and my father and I can't be seen at the airport. Will you do the required maintenance and fly the DC-6 to Panama with my father?"

I smiled back. "I thought you'd never ask."

I worked on the DC-6 with a skeleton maintenance crew to get her ready for the "ferry flight" from Chino to Panama City's Omar Torrijos Herrera International Airport. It took a good month plus to get the white with blue striping bird fixed up because it had been sitting on an airport ramp for quite a long time and was in major disrepair. But I had finally completed all the required maintenance with the exception of re-cowling the number four engine. She was ready to go.

The Plan

The father, HK, who was also an aircraft mechanic like myself, would make the trip to the Chino Airport with me. The two of us would re-cowl the number four engine. Then we'd run all four engines and check all the aircraft systems before the flight. If everything checked out, we would fly the bird to Brownsville, Texas, refuel, then complete the trip to Panama. Upon arrival in Panama we would hand off the DC-6 to the four Mexican nationals and collect the $$$.

The Reality

HK and I arrived at the Chino Airport, and the DC-6 was parked on one of the maintenance ramps. We both donned our mechanic coveralls and began working on the number four engine, ready to install the cowling. All was looking good until a black SUV with government plates pulled up in front of the DC-6. Five men got out. Two were wearing business suits; the other three were wearing green military flight suits. The two MIBs approached me while HK was up on a ladder and under the number four engine. They introduced themselves. One was a DEA agent; the other was an administrator from the local Federal Aviation Administration. And they were not there to help us.

The DEA agent said, "This aircraft is officially impounded by the US Government, and if you try to leave with it, these three gentlemen in flight suits will chase you and shoot you down.

The Doctor was suddenly having a bad day. But the feds standing in front of me didn't know who I was.

I said, "We're just mechanics; we're not pilots. And it would take two pilots and a flight engineer to fly this DC-6."

The DEA agent then asked, "Who hired you?"

I shrugged. "I don't know. They called on the phone and offered us this job and didn't identify themselves."

The DEA agent asked, "How do you get paid? Over the phone too?"

"No. I gave them a mailing address to send the check."

At that the DEA agent said, "Well, finish up your work here. The five of us are going over to Flo's Airport Café. And when we return we're taking possession of this pirate aircraft."

I told him, "We just have to taxi the DC-6 to the run-up pad with the number four engine cowling still off and run it up, then pull the number four engine oil screen and check for metal."

Four of the five men left for Flo's restaurant; the FAA inspector requested to stay with us. He walked over to the ladder HK was still perched on under the number four engine, trying to hide his face.

The agent said, "I know you. You're HK."

HK turned and looked down at the inspector. "Dammed right you know me, and you know this DC-6 is leaving now, with or without a ferry permit."

The FAA inspector laughed as he handed HK the official ferry permit. "Just promise me this aircraft will never return."

Both HK and I smiled and nodded in agreement.

HK and I boarded the DC-6. He climbed into the left captain's seat, and I settled into the right copilot seat. We engaged all four engines and taxied to the run-up pad with the cowlings still off the number four engine and ran all four engines, which checked out. All aircraft systems checked good also.

HK, who was considerably older than me—he was about my dad's age—turned to me, smiling. "Well, kid, you ready to go?"

I grinned. "Roger that."

Chino is a control tower-controlled airport, and on taxi out I called the control tower and gave him our aircraft number. "We're leaving now. Bye!"

On takeoff roll HK said, "Kid, when I say landing gear up, you put the landing gear handle up even if we're still on the ground."

"You got it."

Just about then he said, "Gear up!"

And even though we were still on the takeoff roll, I put the gear handle in the up position just as HK pulled back on the steering column and left the runway. He immediately banked *hard* left to buzz Flo's restaurant on our departure. We passed over no more than fifty feet above the café's roof.

On our turn out I could see the restaurant patrons had emptied out into the parking lot as we had their full attention as well as the DEA agent's attention.

We landed in Brownsville, Texas, and parked next to some aircraft that were used to smuggle electronics from the US into Mexico. We fit right in with the smugglers because they assumed we were doing the same thing. HK and I got the cowlings from the cargo compartment and recowled the number four engine. After fueling the aircraft with one thousand gallons of Avgas, we called it a day and went to the hotel.

The next morning after a hearty breakfast, we boarded the DC-6 and took off for Panama. The flight went as planned, and after landing we were directed to the all-too-familiar military ramp.

It was raining heavily, and I told HK, "I've seen this movie before; this is the part where we go to jail. So let's not open the door until we've had lunch. I'm not going to jail hungry again."

HK and I ate the catering we had brought for the trip then thirty minutes later we opened the door. The aircraft broker with the four Mexican nationals were there waiting, soaking wet.

Oops. Sorry guys.

They handed us a saturated brown paper bag filled with cash. And we said our goodbyes.

HK and I went to my favorite hotel in downtown Panama City; I believe it was a Holliday Inn that had a great bar in the basement. After a very long, hot shower. I went to meet HK in the bar. Walking into the bar, I saw a government agent I recognized. He was an older guy with salt-and-pepper hair and sitting at a table with four younger men.

I sauntered up to the table. "What are you ass-clowns doing here?"

One of the younger agents said, "We're big game fishing."

The older agent and I laughed.

The older agent turned to his associate. "Guys, that story never did work for either side. This is the Doctor; he's one of ours." Then he turned back to me. "We've been tracking your DC-6 since you left Brownsville. The Honduran government wanted to force you down, but when we found out you were flying, we told them the flight was one of ours."

At that I thanked him and bought them all a round of cocktails on me. Then I asked again, "Why *are* you guys here?"

The senior agent said, "Well, your buddy Noriega has told the US to go pound sand one too many times."

"And how's that working out for him?"

"Listen."

The entire time we'd been at the hotel, I was aware of blaring music coming from somewhere in the city; it was so loud you could still hear it there in the basement. It was two songs playing over and over and over again: "You're No Good" by Linda Rondstadt and "These Boots are Made for Walking" by Nancy Sinatra.

The senior agent smiled. "That music was our PSYOPS guys' idea," he said, referring to the psychological operations division. Basically, mind war games. They had positioned four armored personnel carriers— sometimes called battle taxis—mounted with huge speakers and positioned them at the four corners of the Vatican's diplomatic quarters in Panama where Noriega was taking refuge.

HK and I had reservations to fly from Panama to Miami and then onto Los Angeles. During this last adventure, I had made up my mind to officially retire from mercenary flying before I left Panama. While HK and I had one last round of drinks with the agents, I informed the senior agent of that decision.

He nodded. "By the way, we've changed your and HK's flight reservations. You're both flying from Panama directly to LAX. One of our agents will meet you upon your arrival to escort you through Immigration and Customs."

"Why the change of itinerary?" I asked.

The senior agent broke out laughing. "Because the old Customs lady in Miami is still really pissed."

Ha!

As promised, on arrival at LAX we were met by a government agent who walked us through Immigration and Customs with no problems. All he had to do was show his Fed ID. The agent escorted us to a limo waiting curbside to take us to the Wild Goose strip club. We got in and the Fed leaned down.

"Enjoy your retirement, Doctor," he said, then closed the door.

Epilogue: Back at Woody's Wharf, 1989

Officially retired from the mercenary life, I went to work for a DC-8 cargo outfit based out of Ypsilanti, Michigan, called Rosenbalm Aviation. After paying my dues as a copilot, I became a DC-8 Captain. We call these airlines outfits because real airlines have all their aircraft painted the same color. Ha! And as nonsked outfits tend to do, they went bankrupt.

Sooo, after seven more airline outfits—with most going broke—I finally made it to retirement in 2017. I retired as a Boeing B-747 captain. I even flew as captain on the brand new Boeing B-747-8, with both passengers and cargo.

Final fun fact: A steering wheel from one of my crashed DC-3s and a plaque of some of my airline outfit' uniform wings are currently enshrined on the wall of my favorite nonsked bar, the Jet Lag Club in Narita, Japan.

If you make it there, tell the owner, Vincent, and his dog, Inop, I miss them.

#

Unfortunately it took me many, many—did I say many?—years to come to the conclusion. I had used up ten of my nine lives.

I had also learned there was one undeniable fact of life and money: no matter how much money you make, it is directly proportional to what you are spending. Only your lifestyle changes, not your personal net-worth. So take it from me; it's better to have less and not be looking over your shoulder. You only need to lower your survival chest!

When asked what happened to all my women, money, jets, limos, and houses, I like to refer to words of wisdom from W.C. Fields.

I spent half my money on women, gambling, and booze; the other half I wasted.

The Doctor

www.ingramcontent.com/pod-product-compliance
Lightning Source LLC
Chambersburg PA
CBHW031538260326
41914CB00039B/2000/J